CW00539953

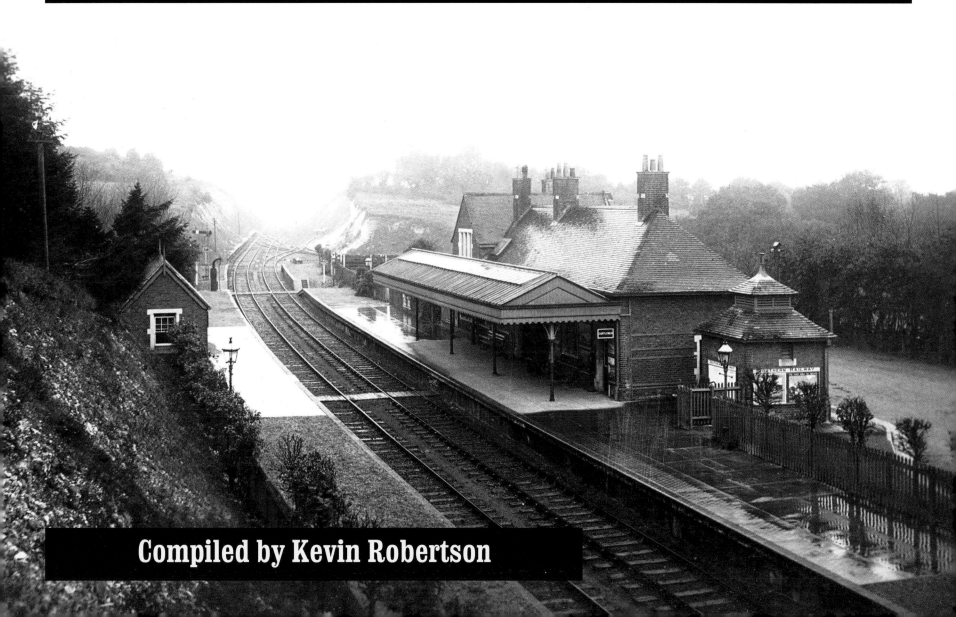

THE MEON VALLEY RAILWAY
Part 2: A Rural backwater

Compiled by Kevin Robertson

ISBN 978-1-906419-68-4

First published in 2012 by Kevin Robertson under the **NOODLE BOOKS** imprint
PO Box 279, Corhampton, SOUTHAMPTON. SO32 3ZX

www.noodlebooks.co.uk

Printed in England by Ian Allan Printing.

Front cover - *Privett. An imaginary scene but based on fact. Drummond's 'Bug' pauses at the down platform, perhaps waiting a crossing. This locomotive and carriage combination was the private means of conveyance for the Locomotive Superintendent of the LSWR, the fearsome Dugald Drummond. Tours of inspection, usually to locomotive facilities under his jurisdiction were made in this fashion, but he was also known to have traversed the MV route on at least four occasions, possibly en-route to Lee-on-the-Solent where he had investment in property.*

From a painting by Craig Tiley

1. Frontispiece - *A wet day at West Meon. The view is undated but taken sometime in Southern Railway days. Already economy has occurred, the footbridge removed - access between the two platforms replaced by a board crossing the position of which is identified by the depression in the platforms. This was deliberately located close by the signal box - so the signalman might keep a wary eye on passengers as they crossed the line. (The signal box is almost out of sight on the down platform shrouded by trees.) In consequence of this alteration, the water column and starting signal for down trains have been re-sited at the end of the foreshortened platform.*

2. Opposite - *Droxford, circa 1903. Tony Williams*

Note - Each image is numbered consecutively throughout this book. Where known, the locations of these images are shown on the map on Page 6.

INTRODUCTION

As with Part 1 in this series, this is a book I have had the greatest of pleasure in compiling. Partly this is because of a local affinity and partly I will admit, because I spend a large amount of time compiling books produced by others (and very enjoyable too) but I had almost forgotten the enjoyment in studying for one's own book.

That said, I have been humbled by the response to the first book in this series. At the time the intention was to try and get away from the sometimes dry railway history (please - certainly not all railway books are produced in such fashion) and present the past in a form, I hope, more acceptable to a modern market. Some of that market do still enjoy sitting down and digesting dates, facts and figures from years ago: others, and I suspect the majority, do not. They might have a mere passing interest, and it is for that reason that I again present with is a primarily pictorial viewpoint.

Again this book attempts to fall into two camps, the railway enthusiast certainly and also the local historian and / or resident of the Meon Valley. In so doing it is not easy to be all things to all people. The enthusiast wants the railway detail, the method of operating, times, engine numbers etc, the local historian probably does not. Consequently if either group feel disadvantaged I apologise, that was never intended to be the case.

As before I have also deliberately stayed away from the 'then and now' imagery. There is of course a place for such works, but in a present day world where 'credit-crunch' is the phrase used in every other sentence, the decision was made to stick with fact. Besides you can still visit West Meon today or walk along the trackbed in various places. (Please respect those parts that are not accessible and especially those stations that now form private houses.)

Even so the amount of available material has resulted in an increase from the anticipated 72 sides to that seen. There has also been a consequential increase in price from the original intention, for that I apologise, both as publisher and author. I do hope the small increase is considered worthwhile.

I am often asked two conflicting questions, one "...where do you get your photographs from?" and the other, "...why have you not included a view of....?". The answer to the first is from friends, contacts, archives and often through word of mouth. This book might be read by someone in an evening yet I can promise the amount of time, travelling, computer / postage / research time involved in the production of any book is considerable. Why not include a view, say of East Tisted (or elsewhere) in 1910 - simply because we do not have one. (If you do have one *PLEASE* let me know!)

It was in consequence of an unsolicited e-mail that the wonderful images on the next two pages appeared. I am confident there are others. Consider also that whilst we nowadays have a globalised network, only a few generations ago it was local cameramen who were recording the scene, often with heavy cumbersome and at times unreliable equipment. They would not know their results until developed later. I would really love to know what happened to such material from all these local individuals.

Many friends old and new have assisted with this work, and it is with grateful thanks that I acknowledge the help and assistance of: Ray Bartlett, Sean Bolan, Pat Butler, Colin Chivers, David Foster-Smith, Gerald Jacobs, John Martin, Kevin Potts, Christopher Purdie, David Monk-Steel, Ray Stone, Denis Tillman, Bob Winkworth, the South Western Circle, Wickham Parish Council, for permission to use material from the Stan Woodford collection, David Wigley, Tony Williams and Alastair Wilson. Plus anyone I have omitted to mention and of course all those whose material is seen and acknowledged. Any errors or omissions are mine alone.

Kevin Robertson. Corhampton 2011

...dow & South Western Railway.
(Meon Valley Railway.

R.T. Relf & Son.
Contractors
Head Office
Plymouth.

Contractors Office
Fareham.
9 April 1908.

Mr W.H. Avery
Dear Sir.

We have pleasure in certifying that you have been employed by us during the past 4½ years. For the first year or so as Civil Engineer on the West-Meon Section of this railway, about 8 miles in length, when you had sole charge of the measuring up for Certificates, setting out the works &c including two tunnels one of which was nearly ¾ mile long. Since which you have acted as our Agent generally on this section to our entire satisfaction. We can certify to your honesty accuracy and energy. Yours faithfully

(Signed) R.T. Relf & Son.

A chance contact after the release of the first volume in the series was with John Martin. An unsolicited note with the attached image on the left hand page (3) commented, "My maternal grand father was William Henry Avery. He was a Contractor Engineer working on the construction of the Meon Valley Railway between 1900 and 1903.". John was unsure of the location, which is clearly West Meon and is also totally different view from any seen before. Further correspondence revealed two further items of interest. The first is seen above (4) and although again unidentified by John, may well be associated with either one of the tunnels, or perhaps a test boring for the viaduct foundations at West Meon. The third item, left is a letter of reference to Mr Avery from the contractor, R T Relf & Sons. Possibly Civil Engineers, such as Mr Avery were engaged on a contractual basis rather than as a full-time member of staff, although it may also have been, that as per the next paragraph, William Avery moved around in pursuance of his career and / or available work. Unknown before is that Relf had a contractor's office at Fareham. As an aside, in 1902 William Avery married a local girl from White Wool, not far from West Meon. John Martin was also able to provide detail of some other railway contracts William Avery worked upon. These were:

1892 - 1897: Served articles as an engineering assistant with Messrs Petrick Brothers, Plymouth.
1897 - 1898: Contractor engineer working for Messrs John Aird & Co on the Marlborough and Grafton Railway.
1900 - 1903: Agent and Contractor engineer working for R T Relf & Son, Plymouth, on the Meon Valley Railway, Fareham to Alton.
1903 - 1906: Contractor engineer working for Walter Scott & Middleton Ltd. on the Cheltenham and Honeybourne Railway.
1907 - 1914: Contractor engineer working for Walter Scott & Middleton Ltd. on the Euston to Watford Railway.
1930 - 1935: Engineer working for Logan & Hemingway on the GWR Westbury loop line.

It is possible, that prior to the formal opening (see notice on page 9), some through goods services may have been deliberately routed over the new line. This was a not uncommon practice with a new railway and would not have required Board of Trade sanction provided passenger services were not involved. The purpose was to assist in the consolidation of earthworks (so also identifying any problems), as well as affording familiarity of operation to locomotive crews and other staff.

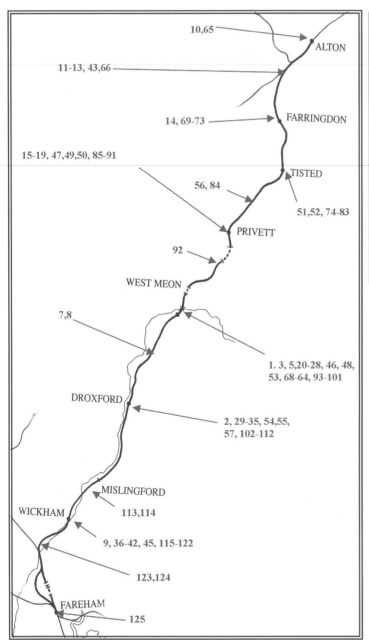

10,65 — ALTON

11-13, 43,66 —

14, 69-73 → FARRINGDON

15-19, 47,49,50, 85-91

TISTED

56, 84 →

51,52, 74-83

PRIVETT

92 →

WEST MEON

7,8

1. 3, 5,20-28, 46, 48, 53, 68-64, 93-101

DROXFORD

2, 29-35, 54,55, 57, 102-112

MISLINGFORD

WICKHAM   113,114

9, 36-42, 45, 115-122

123,124

FAREHAM — 125

The route of the Meon Valley Railway. Figures in red refer to the location, if known, where an image appearing within this book was taken. Map courtesy of Denis Tillman.

5. Above - *West Meon looking north probably taken around the time of the Board of Trade Inspection described opposite. From the illustration the contractors have gone, leaving any finishing off to men of the LSWR who will have provided their own standard fittings and equipment. At this stage gravel ballast covers the sleepers - in later years more conventional granite chippings was common. Two items at least appear to be missing, signals and lamp tops. Possibly the former may not have been visible from this angle, although the apparent lack of windows in the end wall of the signal box could indicate installation was still on-going. Whatever, point rodding run will be seen to be present. Lamp-tops for the platform oil-lamps are similarly absent, a detail that would have been easy to remedy. What gives further credence to the idea this is an image from the 'complete - yet prior to opening period' is the fresh chalk in the cutting beyond the bridge, lack of growth elsewhere and total absence of staff / passengers The fact the trees are also devoid of leaf is another indication. Notice the end of the staff cottages, just visible on the extreme right above the signal box. Similar terraced dwellings were provided by the railway at Tisted, Privett, West Meon and Mislingford at least. The resident station master would occupy the station itself, the cottages provided for either station staff or a member of staff from the permanent-way department. Not commented on within the inspection or elsewhere was the common practice of the contractor, in this case Messrs Relf, being responsible for maintenance of the civil engineering of the railway for 12 months after completion.*

Collection Bob Winkworth

6. Opposite - *Contemporary but undated comic card. Similar cards circulated for any number of railway lines, the names changed to suit. The originals were invariably hand-coloured, the legend a general term and not necessarily representative of travel by a particular route.*

INSPECTION PRIOR TO OPENING

"I have the honour to report for the information of the Board of Trade, that in compliance with the instructions contained in your Minute of the 16th March, I made an inspection on the 2nd and 3rd instants of the new works on the Meon Valley Railway constructed by the L & SW Railway Company.

This line commences by a junction with the Company's Farnham, Alton and Winchester branch at Butts Junction, and has a general S.S.W. direction terminating by a junction with the Company's Bishopstoke & Portsmouth line near Fareham Station.

The total length of the Rly. is 22 miles 24.25 chs.

The authorised limits of lateral and horizontal deviation do not appear to have been exceeded. The line is single throughout except at stations, where loops are provided. The gauge is 4' 8½".

Land has been purchased for a double line and double line overbridges have been built, but some of the underbridges have only been constructed for a single line of way.

The ruling gradient has an inclination of 1 in 90 with a length of 47 chs. The sharpest curve (except at junctions where 20 chs. exist) has a radius of 37 chs., to a length of 33chs.

FORMATION - The width for a single line is 19ft. The space between double lines is 6ft. Between the main line and sidings there is (except at Tisted Stn.) a space of not less than 9½ ft. Between the sides of the widest carriage and any fixed work there is a minimum clearance of 2' 4".

FENCING - Three types are used:
1.   Post with 4 horizontal rails - 4' high.
2.   Post with diagonal rails - 4½' high.
3.   Galvanised wire, -8 wires - 4¼' high.

DRAINAGE - The usual ditches on the higher sides of cuttings and banks have been provided.

PERMANENT WAY - Bullhead rails in 30' lengths, weighing 87 lbs per yd. are laid on C.I. chairs weighing 47 lbs each. The chairs are fastened to ordinary creosoted sleepers by 3 trenails & ⅝" spikes. The sleepers are spaced at 2½' average central intervals. The rails are jointed by bracketed fishplates, weighing 40 lbs per pair. The ballast consists partly of Southampton gravel, & partly of local gravel. The permanent way is in a satisfactory condition, & the line is well ballasted throughout.

EARTHWORKS - For the first 17 miles, the cuttings are carried through chalk with gravel top soil, thence to termination through clay and sand. The heaviest work is to be found between miles 7¾ & 11¼, where there is a length of 20 chs of cutting with a max. depth of 69'. The largest embankment has a length of 59 chs with a max. height of 62'. Slips have occurred about mile 18 in clay cuttings and a retaining wall has been built along the toe of the slope. The movement appears to have been checked. Some of the banks were completed nine months ago and will require careful maintenance.

TUNNELS - There are two of these: - 1 at 7m. 73 ch. Length 1056 yds. constructed for a double line of way; portions of the lining are built in brick in lime mortar and portions in cement concrete. Recesses have been provided on alternate sides at 25 yds intervals. There is no special provision for ventilation. The thickness of brick lining is from 1' 6" to 1' 10½". 2 at 10 ml 32 ch. Length 529 yds. Construction is similar to No. 1. Both these tunnels are carried through chalk, have dry interiors, and show no signs of weakness.

BRIDGING - There are 21 overbridges, three having girder, and the remainder arched spans. In each case there is a single span varying in length from 28 feet to 50 feet. There are 43 underbridges, twenty of which have wrought iron girders or steel troughing spans, and the remainder arched spans. All of the latter has a single span from 9' to 50 feet in length. Of the metal underbridges, one over the River Meon at mile 20-46 has three spans of 27' and 28' and the others have each a single span of from 7' to 51¾' measured on the skew. The abutments and arching in all these bridges is constructed of red brickwork, in some instances faced with blue brickwork; the masonry work has a solid appearance and shows no signs of weakness.

VIADUCTS - There is one of these near West Meon Station at mile 11-17. The length is 77 yards, and it consists of four plate girder spans from 51 to 58

feet in length. The maximum height is 63½ feet. Steep piers on concrete foundations are used. Solid concrete piers were first proposed, but some weakness in foundations was indicated, and the present type of construction was consequently adopted. I could detect no indication of movement in the concrete footings.

I tested the wrought ironwork and steel troughing in the viaduct and underbridges, and found moderate deflections from the engine load, and sufficient theoretical strength has been provided.

CULVERTS - There are 7 of these with spans from 4' to 10'.

LEVEL CROSSINGS - There are 19 level crossings, four of public and 6 of private footpaths, and 9 of occupation roads.

SIDINGS & STATIONS, SIGNALLING etc.

BUTTS JUNCTION - The arrangements at the termination of the new railway were reported after my inspection in May 1901. The only alterations effected have been the removal of a ground disc signal and certain interlocking. The frame in the signal cabin contains 40 levers of which 5 will be spare when the new line is opened, and 1 is a 'push & pull' lever. The company at present have 3 down distant signals referring to the three single lines which junction here. They wish permission to remove two of these distant signals, leaving one only in use. As all down trains have to slow to pick up the train tablet, I see no objection to this proposal which will result in making two more levers spare. The single distant signal could be led by either one of the three sets of stop signals up in front.

FARRINGDON SIDING - at about mile 2½. There is a single set of facing points leading to the sidings. The points are worked from a ground frame containing 4 levers, it is opened by the train tablet for the section.

TISTED STATION - There is a loop line here for passing trains, and two platforms. On one platform there is a shelter for passengers and on the other a booking hall, ladies room and conveniences for both sexes. The platforms are 200 yds long and 3 feet high and are connected by means of a footbridge. On account of the rising gradient 1 in 100, it will be necessary to place all down trains in sidings clear of the main line before shunting operations are commenced, and a siding long enough to contain the longest trains has been provided for the purpose. The frame in the signal cabin contains 23 levers of which 5 are spare.

PRIVETT STATION - at 7m 34 chs. The arrangements at this station are similar as regards accommodation etc as at Tisted. All up trains will in this case have to be placed in sidings before shunting is commenced, and a siding for the purpose has been provided. The frame in the signal cabin contains 25 levers of which 6 are spare.

WEST MEON STATION - at 11miles 42 chs. Similar arrangement and accommodation as for the last named stations. The frame in the signal cabin contains 25 levers of which 6 are spare. At this place the parish clerk presented me with a petition from the parish council. I inspected the spot where danger was anticipated, and in my opinion the danger has always been in existence owing to a sharp turn in the public road. I do not think there are grounds for any action by the Board of Trade.

DROXFORD STATION - at 15 miles 29 chs. Accommodation is provided as at the other stations. Up trains in view of the rising gradient must be placed in sidings before shunting is commenced, and provision for this has been made. The frame in the signal cabin contains 24 levers of which 5 are spare.

MISLINGFORD SIDING - at 18m 40 A single connection leading to the sidings, which is worked from a ground frame containing 4 levers, opened by the train tablet for the section. In this case if Up trains using the siding cannot be contained within the limits of the flat gradient of 1/330, the train must be placed within the siding points before shunting operations are commenced.

WICKHAM STATION - at 20 miles 39 chs. Similar accommodation as at other stations. It will be necessary to place a down train in the siding provided for the purpose, before shunting operations are commenced. The frame in the signal cabin contains 24 levers of which 6 are spare.

KNOWLE JUNCTION - The southern termination of the new single line terminates with a double junction with the Portsmouth main line between Fareham and Botley Stations. The signal cabin is new, it will replace a former block post known as Knowle Siding from which an old siding connection is at present worked. This old connection will, after the opening of the new line, be worked from a ground frame containing 5 levers all in use, which is bolt-locked from Knowle Junction signal cabin. A new crossover road has also been provided. The frame in the new signal cabin contains 25 levers of which 6 are spare.

The interlocking all these ground frames and signal cabins is correct.

It will be necessary to fix lamps, and clocks at all the stations before opening the new line for traffic, and the connections with signals and points will have to be made, and existing trap points removed, also a temporary watering arrangement at Wickham. The new railway is equipped for single line working by the electric tablet system, and I found the necessary tablet instruments installed at Butts Junction, Tisted, Privett, West Meon, Droxford, and Wickham stations and at Knowle Junction. The Company should submit the necessary undertaking as regards the method of working. Subject to the receipt of this undertaking, and to the proper completion of the works referred to, I can advise the Board of Trade to authorize this new railway for passenger traffic."

Sgnd. Major J W Pringle.

LONDON & SOUTH WESTERN RAILWAY.

INSTRUCTION No. 22, 1903.

Instructions to District Superintendents, Station Masters, Inspectors, Enginemen, Guards, Signalmen, and all others concerned, as to the

OPENING OF THE

MEON VALLEY LINE,

ON

MONDAY, 1st JUNE, 1903,

FOR

PASSENGERS, PARCELS & GOODS TRAFFIC.

This New Line is 22¼ miles in length, and connects with the Alton and Winchester Line at Butts Junction, near Alton Station, and with the Eastleigh and Portsmouth Line at Knowle Junction, between Botley and Fareham Stations.

There are five intermediate Stations, viz. :—Tisted (for Selborne), Privett, West Meon, Droxford (for Hambledon) and Wickham, at each of which there is accommodation for dealing with Horses, Carriages, and Live Stock ; and Sidings for Goods Traffic. Facilities for dealing with Goods and Cattle Traffic are also provided at Faringdon Siding (between Butts Junction and Tisted Station) and Mislingford Siding (between Droxford and Wickham Stations) ; and 5-ton Cranes have been provided at each of the Stations and Sidings.

It is a Single Line throughout, of this Company's standard gauge, with Loops at each of the five Stations.

The Line will be worked under the Train Tablet System (Tyer's No. 6 Instruments), as described in Instruction No. 21, 1903, and the Tablet Sections will be as under :—

Butts Junction to Tisted ;
Tisted to Privett ;
Privett to West Meon ;
West Meon to Droxford ;
Droxford to Wickham ;
Wickham to Knowle Junction.

*The lack of ceremony is indicated also by the lack of photographs from the opening day. Just three have been located, all of indifferent quality. 7. **Top right** - purported to be the first train, an Up working near Meonstoke. It is just possible to discern waving from the carriage windows. 8. **Middle right** - the return working, probably in the same location. 9. **Bottom right** - A Down train at Wickham on the initial day. The locative is an Adams 'Radial' tank.*
Wickham Parish Council: Stan Woodford collection.

Without any apparent ceremony or celebration, the Meon Valley Railway opened to passenger traffic on 1 June 1903. The original opening date was reported to have been set for 25 March, but had been delayed apparently due to signalling and trackwork, the latter particularly at Butts Junction. (Substitution of the distant signals referred to in Maj. Pringle's report perhaps?) Whatever, it could even be concluded the LSWR were not in any particular hurry, indicated also by the lack of occasion on 1 June. (A private party was held at Warnford House on the day, those attending taking a trip on the railway during the afternoon. It is not believed the participants were connected with the LSWR.) June 1 was also the Whitson Bank-holiday Monday and in consequence the railway offered travellers a free single ticket from one station to the next. The return, however, had either to be paid for or recourse made to walking!

10. Left - *Alton seen from the south end with a Waterloo to Southampton service awaiting departure. For those with an amount of time to spare this was a most leisurely route to take amounting also to at least an extra hour on the journey. The image dates from before July 1937 at which time electrification arrived at Alton from Farnham.*

11. Above - *Reported as a down local freight between Alton and Butts Junction seen in Southern Railway days behind a member of the Adams 0395 class.*

12. Opposite top - *Up Meon Valley train leaving the branch at Butts Junction and crossing what was then the start of the double line to Alton.*

13. Opposite top - *From ground level, a view that appeared in the Southern Railway Magazine and reported as unique as being the only place where three single lines branch off a double line: left to Fareham, straight-on to Winchester, and right to Basingstoke. The view was credited to the daughter (no name given) of Signalman Brambler of Butts Junction.*

14. Opposite bottom - *Farringdon Siding* towards Alton. Goods were handled here from the outset although it was not until 1 May 1931 that a passenger platform was provided. The design of goods shed was similar to that provided elsewhere on the line. Here and at Wickham the goods shed contained a 30cwt crane.*

* The railway seem to have had difficulty in reconciling the spelling here with 'Faringdon' used on occasions.

It is regretted, but no early views of Tisted have so far been found.

PRIVETT

15. Top left - *Privett, from the Southern Railway Magazine of December 1923. The trap point in the former loop was provided during the rationalisation of June 1922.*

16 - Top right - *The station and 'the 'Privett Bush' PH viewed from the new road to Basing Park house. No coal merchants were listed as working from Privett although in the early years at least Ralph Trimmer worked from neighbouring Tisted and may have also operated from an office and staithes here as well. History has it the name 'West Tisted' was considered as the name for the stopping place - the village of that name being about the same distance from the railway as Privett. It was rejected due to obvious confusion. Although not referred to, it is probable that any thought of using the name 'Basing', after Mr Nicholson's nearby Basing Park estate, was similarly rejected.*

17 - Bottom left - *From the 1903 RAILWAY MAGAZINE article on the new railway a view of Privett as built. The goods shed will be noted. Apart from at Farringdon and Wickham this is one of the few views of a goods shed at the intermediate stations - although all were originally so provided. Due to limited traffic it is possible they were removed as a maintenance economy. The footbridge will also be seen. Little if any advertising evidence supports the fact this was a station.*

18 - Bottom right - *Privett, together with a ground plan (the latter opposite bottom), featured in an article on the commerce of the Southern Railway during the 1920s. It was described as a "Station in a Rural District"....opened in 1903 designed to serve a very small town or village and surrounding rural district. The accommodation has proved adequate at each of the several stations constructed to this design, and no structural alteration or variation of original design has been found necessary at either place."*

19. - *Privett towards Alton (purported to be one of a series: we would love to see the others!) The view may be dated sometime between 1903 and 1922: the latter time when the loop and signalling were removed. Exactly what is going on is unclear, but it could be affixing a smoke trough as per that protecting the bridge on the down line. Two ladders have been lashed together with rope whilst it will be noted the home signal has been lowered to admit the passage of a down train.*

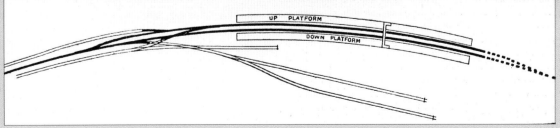

UP PLATFORM

DOWN PLATFORM

WEST MEON

20. - *West Meon at and a few years after opening: notice the difference in the chalk cutting beyond the overbridge. Of those seen (top) most appear to be wearing uniforms applicable to railway work. The exceptions are the two women but could these even be family members? Four men and a boy are indicative of being from the traffic department, the last named close by a barrow on which the station name is recorded. Some commercial traffic, barrels and boxes, await collection / delivery. Beyond the foot and road bridges may just be glimpsed the water column, West Meon the mid-way point on the line and the only place where locomotive water supplies were available.*

21. *The same view, but, and as referred to above, slightly later in years. (It is perhaps a pity that at West Meon various photographers all totally independent of each other, displayed little imagination when selecting a location from which to record their image.) A plethora of posters boards and other advertisements now abound although the staffing level may well have been reduced as only three men are seen.*

STATION MASTERS AT WEST MEON	
c1907	Albert Hardy
c1911-1914	William Burgess Ward
1914-1919	W H Butler
c1920-1922/23*	Luke Partridge
1928-1933	W J Gard
c1937	A Reynalds
c1954	Mr Ward

It is believed the station master post may have been abolished for a while after 1923 but was reinstated later with the post-holder taking charge of the whole line. At some stage circa 1935, the SM post at Wickham was also reinstated.

STATION MASTERS AT TISTED	
c1916*-1922	H N Ewings

STATION MASTERS AT PRIVETT	
c1916*1922	F C Delia

Circa 1922 post removed. *May have been in post for some time beforehand.

22. and 23. - *Viewed from Station Road overbridge looking south towards Droxford, two views, taken a few years apart, possibly c1904 and c1910. In the top view the colossal expanse of chalk it was necessary to remove from the station site and yardage area is apparent - interesting to note also that beyond the station the cutting slope on the left was clearly completed some time before that on the right: as witness the growth on the side. It is of course also possible that slippage had occurred necessitating the removal of further material on the right hand side and / or additional space was deemed necessary for a revised track layout. In the lower view trains are forming a morning crossing, both formed of slightly different LSWR 'block-sets'.* This image also confirms that both tender and tank locomotives were in use on the line. The change in greenery, not just on the far cutting sides but almost throughout the site is apparent. Apart from the train(s) it is apparent that in both views there is a distinct lack of patronage, both passenger and goods. Indeed apart from one individual, presumably the guard of the down train, the station is seemingly deserted, not perhaps what might be expected with two passenger trains in the station - the horse just visible in the yard may be a carriage awaiting trade. The lack of goods traffic in the yard has been commented upon, although it must be said that at certain times, particularly during harvest, West Meon could yield reasonable agricultural revenue.*

* Reference to available timetables has failed to reveal a known booked crossing of passenger trains at West Meon in the years 1903-1914. That is not to say it was not a regular feature. The alternative conclusion was that one of the trains seen was running 'out of course' and this was a delayed or even special working.

24 - *From platform level towards Droxford.* **25** - *Probably soon after opening. The gap in the cutting on the right hand side accommodated nothing more important than a dead end headshunt: a somewhat extravagant provision. At platform level the extent of the paved area of platform is apparent, such restriction applied on both platforms and was similarly replicated at the other stations. No doubt an economy feature, outside the paved area, the surface was of fine chippings.*

26 - *From the south end a view of the yard is available. West Meon was the only station / yard not located on a gradient - special instructions were printed in the Appendices for elsewhere. Goods accommodation was similar at all the stations with two sidings, one including cattle pens and an end loading ramp, as well as a headshunt. To add complication, all five passenger stations also has a scissors crossover. The railway cottages can be seen above the signal box fronting Station Road, near these was also the water storage tank supplying the water columns.*

27 - *Passengers awaiting the arrival of a down train. Two local diary farmers sent milk from the station whilst the Portsea Island Co-operative also owned two farms in the area. It is reported* milk was always sent south to Portsmouth by passenger train from West Meon: in which case the two churns seen were returning empties.*

28 - *A final view in LSWR days. Although once again devoid of passengers - and staff - the yard at least shows some sign of business. Not seen in any of the other images is the 5 ton yard crane with a 16' lift (a similar item was provided at all the stations as well as at Farringdon and Mislingford), there is also a view of a wooden hut alongside the gates the purpose of which is not known. One advantage of the railway was a reduction in the price of coal, then the principal household fuel, to the area. Not surprisingly both here and at the other stations coal was one of the principal sources of traffic. In 1907 for example, the Colliery Supply Co. is listed as having staithes at the station. By 1909 a merchant, I W Knight is shown but this entry disappears afterwards. Another merchant operating at an unreported time was Isaac Abram. In the final years Ray Stone was the merchant at the station.*

* South Western Circle Portfolio notes.

DROXFORD

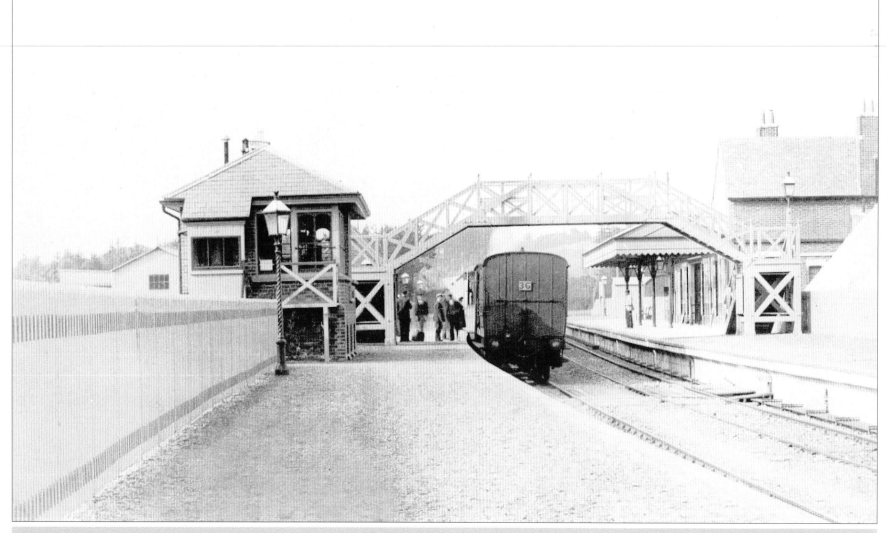

29. - *Pristine Droxford with a train for Alton shortly to depart, note the goods shed in the background. Compare also with Privett and it would appear that smoke troughs may not have been originally fitted to any of the footbridges - they are certainly missing here.*

30. - *Slightly later in years, as witness the shrubs in front of both the fencing and signal box. As built, Droxford served what would now be referred as a 'catchment' area of some 2,000 persons taking in not just the village after which the station was named, but also Soberton, Meonstoke, Corhampton, and Exton. Hambledon, some 3½ miles south east, afforded a further 2,000 people. Whilst excavating for the station in 1900, bones and spearheads were found in an area that later became the station master's garden. (Subsequent digging 75 years later revealed a site thought to date from 450 to 550 AD.) The station was popular with race goers who would travel for the annual meeting at the local course at the start of every May. This continued until just before WW1. (For many years there was also a point-to point meeting for the Hambledon Hunt.)*

SOUTHERN RAILWAY.
(4/31)   (787)
FROM WATERLOO TO
DROXFORD

STATION MASTERS AT DROXFORD	
c1907*-1911	Frank Wills
1916-1917	W Mitchell
1918-1919	A Phillips
1922	E A Cobley
1923-1927	Arthur Powell

*May have been in post for some time beforehand.
By 1931 post removed - although this may have occurred earlier.

31. - *Unfortunately no images of the yard at Droxford in early days have survived. In general terms Droxford would have handled traffic of all types from agricultural goods out, to feedstuffs in as well as the requirements for the local stores. (Grimsby fish for local consumption was a particular traffic but was no doubt also received at all the other stations as well.) This railway monopoly of traffic lasted until the 1920s when there was a gradual switch to road. In 1907 coal was received at the station by Harry May from the Coal Supply Company, although by 1911 the firm of I W Knight (the same as at West Meon) is mentioned., By 1923 it was Read & Sons whilst around the same time the name J E Smith (Portsmouth) Ltd is mentioned. This company operated its own railway wagons but were most likely lettered with Portsmouth as the home station. It is reported that at times 300-400 tons of coal would be stacked in the yard.*

32. - Top left and 33. - Bottom left - Admiral Sir Frederick Charles Doveton Sturdee (1859-1925) returning to Droxford sometime after his victory over a German naval squadron at the battle of the Falklands in December 1914. Apart from the interest in the local dignitaries, railway matters may be served by noticing in the background to No 32 a water tower. Clearly on railway property its purpose was to provide water for the station and railway cottages, it was still standing in the 1950s. Another prominent Droxford resident was Admiral Jellicoe. On one occasion when said personage arrived at the station by train, fog-signals (detonators) were set off whilst his own road coach was pulled down to the village by the villagers themselves.

34. - Top right - Men from the 5th Isle of Wight 'Princess Beatrice's' Volunteer Brigade, Hants, formed up on Station Road, 21 May 1904.

Station Hotel
Droxford

35. - *Station Hotel, Droxford, although to be strictly more accurate, the location for both the railway station and hotel should be in the parish of Brockbridge. (Station Road is seen on the right, a new road provided by the railway as the route of the old road was buried under the railway formation.) To the left the road heads towards Hambledon whilst behind it drops down under the railway. The actual station is but a few yards along Station Road. Built as a private venture, presumably at the same time as the railway, Droxford was the only station to boast such a hotel facility although there would already have been hotels in Wickham and public house accommodation available near the other stations. The facility may well have come about in the hope of attracting race-goers visiting the nearby course, although meetings at Droxford are believed to have been limited. Another possible revenue may have been those attending various hunting and shooting meetings on the estates in the area - some guest to which would not doubt also have been accommodated on the estates themselves. Whatever, despite a no doubt limited trade emanating from the railway, the building has survived and although subject to various name changes, particularly in recent years, remains open today. Droxford / Brockbridge was also the destination of two proposed extensions of the existing branch from Bishops Waltham. The first in 1899 would have resulted in a terminus at Droxford, the second in 1899, a connection into the then proposed Meon Valley line. Both were private ventures rather than being sponsored by the LSWR with the promoters unable to raise the necessary funding.*

36. - *An undated image of Wickham looking north probably soon after opening and originally produced by 'Clark's Cash Stores' in the town. As was typical for the period the ballast (see page 7) covers the sleepers. Churns abound - again presumably empty, whilst the trolley is stacked with the sacks.*

37. - *A few years later and the site has taken on a more mature appearance, the ballast less prominent and a board crossing evident between the platforms. As with the other stations, the staple traffic of coal appears to have been in the hands of several businesses over the years. The first name mentioned, although without a date, is H T Clements who also dealt in corn. Similar business was undertaken by Edney Bros. By 1927 it was Wm. Fred. Churcher although this operation ceased by 1931. Subsequent to this date Mrs Flora Bailey handled coal in the town but not it appears at the station. After this time it is likely then that either outside companies delivered coal locally or this may even have been handled by general merchants.*

STATION MASTERS AT WICKHAM			
? -1923	A Foster	1935-1939*	Fred. Wiltshire
1927	Oscar Churcher	c1948-1955	W F Squire
1931	W F Churcher		
*Mr Wiltshire may have been in post for part, at least, of WW2			

MEON VALLEY (ALTON AND FAREHAM) LINE.

No. 224.—The Engineer will have possession of the undermentioned Electric Train Tablet Circuits, on the dates and between the times shewn, for the purpose of cleaning and overhauling the Electric Train Tablet instruments :—

Electric Train Tablet Section.	Date and Hours.	Remarks.
West Meon and Droxford.	From 9.45 a.m. on **Monday, 22nd June,** until completed the same day.	**Mr. Ward, West Meon,** to arrange pilot working.
Droxford and Wickham.	From 9.45 a.m. on **Tuesday, 23rd June,** until completed the same day.	**Mr. Mitchell, Droxford,** to arrange pilot working.
Wickham and Fareham East.	From 10.0 a.m. on **Wednesday, 24th June,** until completed the same day.	**Mr. Foster, Wickham,** to arrange pilot working.

Pilot working to be carried out in accordance with Regulation No. 27, of the Standard Block Regulations for Single Lines worked on the Electric Train Tablet system.

38. Left and **39. Above** - *Staff views at Wickham and with some obvious similarity in those depicted between the two. In the left hand view there would appear to be the station master (Mr Foster), possibly a clerk (extreme right) with a porter (witness the cap badge) standing nearest the canopy support - possibly this man may also have been a porter/signalman. The others wearing uniform may have been junior members within the porter grade. In the right hand view the man seated on the right of the trolley has the distinct look of a gamekeeper. Whatever, whilst appreciating Wickham may well have had potentially more staff than the other stations, by taking an average of four traffic department personnel at each and two at Farringdon this reveals a total of 22-24 employed. On top of this would be permanent way staff, perhaps another 30, plus a proportionate claim on time of those who might only visit on occasions, bridge inspectors, painters, relaying gangs, etc etc. On top of all this would be the train crews.*
Both - Wickham Parish Council, Stan Woodford collection.

40. Top left - *Wickham looking north. As referred to at image No. 26, working instructions dictated that a down goods train must be placed in the siding clear of the running line before shunting work is commences. The presence then of the brake van on the running line would mean the hand brake was securely applied.*

41. Top right - *An Adam's Jubilee on what may be a through train from Waterloo to Gosport.*

42. Left - *A final view north, this time in Southern Railway days - notice the difference in colour scheme for the 'Gentlemen' sign compared with that seen at No. 38.*

WINTER........

In late December 1927, the Meon Valley line, along with the Mid Hants route - and further afield the line to Amesbury and Bulford, were severely affected by what would be described as 'The Great Snowstorm'. Its effect on the railway was vividly told in the *SOUTHERN RAILWAY MAGAZINE* shortly afterwards, by P Hatch, the Alton station master.

"This story is dedicated to the enginemen working the Meon Valley Line, who, driving undauntedly through enormous snow drifts with regulators hard over, were thrown from side to side of their footplates, drenched with fine snow, deafened by huge icicles dropping from tunnels upon their engine cabs, snowed up, pulled out by assistant engines, stood in snow to their waists clearing snow from ash pans and oiling holes, emerged triumphant minus head lamps, discs and sidesteps, and kept the line open for traffic, and with them must be mentioned the stationmaster who rendered such valuable assistance between Farringdon Siding and West Meon Station. To the enginemen working the snow ploughs and material trains on the Mid Hants, line, who, exposed to the utmost fury of the gale, as their engines could not be turned, drove into 20ft. drifts, foot by foot, day by day, until they in turn were snowed in, dug out, retreated to clear drifts accumulated behind them, forward once more, again driven back, again forward, almost blinded and frozen with the force of the hurricane, literally smashed their way through to Winchester Junction on the 29th day of December, 1927.

"To the Engineer's Permanent Way Staff, lead by the Divisional Engineer, in person, and his wonderful Inspectors, who met at Farnham on the night of December 26th, prepared to travel via Brookwood to commence clearing Mid Hants line at the Winchester Junction end, were ordered to Basingstoke instead to clear the tremendous drifts there, worked all night until noon the following day, then proceeded to Winchester Junction to carry out the original arrangement. Submerged in snow to their shoulders, blinded and frozen by the fearful blizzard, they worked, suffered (and hungered, too) and eventually succeeded in performing the most herculean feat of endurance known to their own, or any other department in the Company's service.

"To the operating District Inspectors, and the whole of the operating staffs at the stations named below, who worked long hours, with hands and feet nearly frozen, and, when the thaw set in, with water running out of their boots, and did not cease their strenuous efforts until the glad news was received that normal working would commence on the Mid Hants Line on Wednesday, January 4th, 1928.

"Special mention must be made of the signalman at Itchen Abbas who waded through the fearful drifts to Winchester Junction to fetch the tablet, and again to the snow plough to fetch assistance for the train snowed in between Alresford and Ropley, each journey being performed in total darkness, and last, but not least, to the Commercial Staff at Alton who dealt so ably with the rush of telephone work, especially during the time when the other lines were down.

"Insert the point of a compass in the Southern Railway Company's map midway between Micheldever and Bentworth, and draw a circle embracing Alton, Tisted, Privett, West Meon, Medstead, Ropley, Alresford, Itchen Abbas and Winchester, then up to Basingstoke, and across the Basingstoke and Alton Light Railway, and you will see at a glance, the track of the greatest snow storm in living memory, which visited the county of Hampshire on December 25th, 1927, and two following days.

"CHRISTMAS DAY - Snow commenced to fall about 6.0 p.m. Christmas Day, and continued unceasingly the two. following days, accompanied by a bitter wind of great velocity. The Mid Hants Line, Alton to Winchester Junction, suffered severely, snow piling up in 10, 15 and 20ft. drifts in places, the Basingstoke and Alton Light Railway was completely blocked, whilst the Meon Valley Line, Alton to Fareham, had deep drifts at Farringdon Siding, Privett, and West Meon.

"BOXING DAY, DECEMBER 26th. - The outlook on Boxing morning, December 26th, was very serious. The 7.46 a.m. Eastleigh to Waterloo had passed into the single line at Winchester Junction and disappeared. Wires were down between Winchester and Woking, and between Woking and Alton on Winchester circuit, so that stationmasters in the stricken area could not communicate direct with Head Office, Waterloo, such messages having to be transmitted *via* Alton. All signals were drooping with the weight of snow, and when freed, froze to the on position, so that trains had to be handsignalled past them.

"Points and ground discs were very faulty, in spite of the strenuous efforts of the platelayers, who used 5cwt. of salt per day at Alton alone, and worked like Trojans, too. It was a battle between the snow and men's endurance, and for the first two days the snow was the victor.

"News filtered through the signal box circuit about 8.30 a.m. that the 7.46 a.m. ex Eastleigh was completely snowed in, between Winchester Junction and Itchen Abbas, as the funnel of the engine could just be discerned, and through the same source, it was later ascertained that the stationmaster at Winchester was endeavoring to get the passengers out and worked back to Winchester, which operation he accomplished after a terrible struggle, the snow being 20ft. deep in places. He also sent a message *via* Alton asking for at least 50 men to dig out the train.

"In the light of these events it was certain that no train could pass through the Mid Hants line that day, and arrangements were made accordingly to run a shuttle service between Alresford .and Alton commencing with the

9.49 a.m. from Alton and returning from Alresford at 11.54 a.m., arriving Alton 12.44 p.m. These trains had great difficulty in getting through.

"Another effort was made by 1.42 p.m. from Alton which reached Alresford, after a terrific struggle, but could not get back. This part of the story is best related in the words of the Alresford stationmaster: "*Train left on return journey at 3.10 p.m., returning to Alresford a few minutes later as cutting was blocked by fall of snow and earth. The obstruction was removed, but the weather conditions becoming rapidly worse, the engine was detached and ran through to Ropley to clear the line, and render it possible for train to proceed. The snow, however, had drifted so deeply that it was considered unsafe to make the attempt, train was therefore berthed at Alresford and engine sent home light about 5.0 p.m.*"

"This was the last movement made on the Mid Hants. Line that day. Meanwhile, motorists and road transport people were struggling through the snow, up to their armpits, into Alresford, Ropley, Medstead, and Alton stations, leaving their cars and lorries deeply embedded in snow drifts on the London and Winchester main road, the waiting rooms at the-three last-named stations

43. - The cutting between Alton and Butts Junction.

being kept open all night to accommodate stranded passengers, as once they gained admission, they could not leave, owing to the inclement weather. The Alresford passengers were accommodated at local hotel.

"An incident which occurred during the first night's vigil at Alton was related to the station-master on Tuesday morning, December 27th. It appears that two belated motorists staggered into the warm waiting room, about 3.0 a.m. that morning, having waded through snow up to their waists, from somewhere unknown, they could not say, and dropped down upon the first stool, and slept the sleep of utter exhaustion until 7.0 a.m., when they rallied sufficiently to leave by first up train to London at 7.35 a.m. One wonders what would have happened to those gentlemen if the waiting room had been closed.

HIGH WALKING! -Another incident occurred at Ropley, where a gentleman wading across the fields, as he thought, caught his foot in someone's clothes line and fell down. He could not see that he was walking across the garden belonging to a house close by.

"During this time the Permanent Way Department had not been idle. They were doing everything possible to get a gang of men together at Farnham for a Ballast Train, to dig out the 7.46 from Eastleigh, their difficulties being considerably increased by the fact that every available platelayer was busily engaged in his own district keeping the points, etc., free from snow and all shopmen were on holiday and could not be secured. After superhuman efforts, however, the Chief Permanent Way Inspector at Guildford succeeded in getting a gang in readiness which, at the last moment, was ordered to Basingstoke, as the main lines there were completely blocked with snow. There they worked, hungry and frozen until noon the following day, afterwards proceeding to Winchester.

TUESDAY, DECEMBER 27th. - The morning of December 27th, 1927, commenced with shrieking wind and blinding snow. Signals and points put out of action almost as soon as platelayers had cleared them, an urgent S.O.S. made to D.O.S.O. 2208 for salt from all stations, which was promptly attended to in spite of the fact that the stores department was closed for the Christmas Holidays. Messrs. Richards and Anderson were directing operations at 2208.

"England's greatest poet is credited with having said "Troubles cometh not singly but in battalions", and as the bad news came through this bitter morning we would have believed him if he had said something worse. The 7.46 a.m. Eastleigh was still snowed in at Winchester Junction, the Basingstoke and Alton line still blocked and the Mid Hants. Line now completely blocked. In addition the 4.50 a.m. Waterloo to Gosport was stuck in a huge drift near Tisted blocking the Meon Valley Line. Two engines were immediately requested from Guildford to force a passage through the Mid Hants. Line, as far as Alresford, leaving Alton at 9.40 a.m. Good progress was made at first, the engines clearing to Ropley, leaving that station I may tell you it was a marvel how we got through to Alresford for 10.16 a.m., but bad luck pursued them, and they could not get through.

"A third engine sent to their assistance fared no better, the three becoming snowed in, and after being dug out, with the villagers' assistance, the attempt was abandoned, the engines returning to Alton at 3.50 p.m. Better progress was made on Meon Valley Line, the West Meon stationmaster telephoning that the 4.50 a.m. ex Waterloo had been pulled out of the drift at Tisted, but ran into another one at West Meon, again assisted out, eventually getting through to Fareham, and opening up the Meon Valley Line. This was excellent news, and cheered when Winchester advised us. On the engines the crews were soaked with the snow thrown up in clouds as they pushed through. Later, at 7.0 p.m. the 7.46 Eastleigh train was finally dug out and pulled back to Winchester.
"WEDNESDAY, DECEMBER 28th. Wednesday, December 28th, from a weather point of view was no improvement upon the previous two days, the Meon Valley Line was still open, it is true, but drivers were experiencing terrible difficulties in getting through.

To give readers some idea of the fight the enginemen put up, driver Moseley's experiences are now relayed in his own words. *"Leaving Gosport Station with the 7.35 am train, plodding our way through about a foot of snow, great care had to be taken as points and signals were frozen, some being in the all-right position and others at danger, those in the latter position having to be practically disregarded and hand signals taken, as I did not know whether they had been pulled by the signalman or were frozen. All went fairly well until Droxford was reached, then the trouble began. The drifts began to get thicker but we still struggled on. The first big drift was encountered at the mouth of the West Meon tunnel, being quite 6ft. deep, having a great struggle but we still pressed on, clearing this one, but was not allowed to go far before we found ourselves in another one, and still getting thicker. On entering Privett tunnel, the prettiest sight I ever saw were the icicles hanging down very thick and from 6 to 8ft. long, the train striking them and snapping them off they fell on the engine like bricks from the roof of the tunnel. Well, after emerging from there another big drift was encountered but we still kept ploughing on, and I may tell you it was a marvel how we did get through. After this it was fair sailing until leaving Tisted, when worse trouble was in store for us, running into two very large banks of snow, one near Tisted Station the other near Farringdon Goods Siding, this one being 8 or 10 feet deep. I was travelling at 50 to 55 miles an hour, the shock as the engine struck the snow threw my fireman and myself from one side of the footplate to the other. I flew to the regulator and gave her all the steam I possibly could, and by doing so I just managed to crawl through with about 6in of snow on the footplate, and to make matters worse, I could neither see out of the eyeglass or look over the side as the snow was ploughing up in clouds, wetting us both through. After that it was fairly good travelling*

except of course, about 18in of snow on the rail. On reaching Alton the engine was like a block of snow, every oil-hole and motion and wheels were completely blocked. After this experience another shock was awaiting us - the passengers were looking and taking stock of the snow on the engine when one, a bit more quick-sighted than the others, though he saw blood underneath as I was moving down to the water column and he at once sent and reported it to the stationmaster who came and asked me if I knew I had blood on the engine. Of course I looked around the best I could, but saw nothing. This caused me to crawl under the engine in about 18in of snow, but I saw nothing, so he went and found the passenger

44. - *SR 1927, exact location uncertain.*

who had reported it to come and show me where it was, and to my relief he pointed to the only strip of red paint that was visible about a foot long on the Spectacle plate, the rest being covered with snow. And now for one more incident which occurred on the return journey. Passing Faringdon goods siding, we ran into another big drift and being bunker first the snow entered the ash-pan, and completely blocking all draught to the fire, I could therefore, get no steam, and had another good time at Privett crawling under he engine in about 2ft. of snow with coal pick and rake to clear this, being bound to do so to get steam. I do not think I will say any more or I shall fill a book, I may add this was the worst week I ever experienced in my 37 years' service on the footplate."

"Driver Moseley's experience was typical of that of every driver on the Meon Valley Line, and as the full passenger: and goods service was maintained from this date onwards in that section, we will transfer our attention to the Mid Hants. Line. The Divisional Engineer and his Inspectors had arranged to fight the drifts both ends, commencing to-day with the assistance of men recruited from Guildford shops.

"Three engines coupled with snow plough passed into the single line at Butts Junction at 8.5 a.m., followed by another engine and van with a gang of men at 1.0 p.m., a ballast train coming in at the Winchester Junction end at the same time.

"The drifts were so deep that the plough could not advance through the second cutting from Alresford, but having cleared Alresford it was decided to run a special from that station to Alton, and the provision of the train, together with the misfortune that befell it, is best told by the stationmaster at Alresford.

"A train consisting of engine, coach and van was made up, the passengers for various places such as Bournemouth, Eastleigh, who had been stranded at Alresford since Monday afternoon were delighted at the prospect of at last being able to continue their journey, even though it was by such a roundabout route as *via* Woking. The train left at 3.10 p.m., but fate was against it. At 4.30 p.m. the fireman was back reporting the train stuck in the snow about 2 miles away. All available assistance was sent to endeavor to dig it out, the signalman at Itchen Abbas carried a message to the Inspector in charge of the snow plough asking for immediate assistance. Unfortunately the plough was also in difficulties, it was only by extraordinary exertion on the part of the men with it that they were able to get back to Alresford by 7.40 p.m. The plough at once went forward to assist the snowed up train, but it was not until after 10.0 p.m. that the train arrived at Ropley and then only with the assistance of another engine sent from Alton to pull it through the last drift near Ropley Station. Upon arrival at Alton at 10.50 p.m., the half-frozen passengers were changed into a well heated train which left for Woking at 11.14 p.m., and one gentleman specially thanked the station-master on behalf of the other passengers, for the heroic efforts of the engineer's department men who had dug out their train from the fearful drifts between Ropley and Alresford.

THURSDAY, DECEMBER 29th. - The bitter wind somewhat abated today, and the snow plough with three engines coupled, again entered the single line at Butts Junction shortly after 10.0 a.m., an engine and van with another gang of men following at 11.15 a.m. Two short trains were worked from Alton to Alresford at 2.55 p.m. and 6.35 p.m., and arrived back at Alton from Alresford at 4.52 p.m. and 8.40 p.m. This was the red letter day of that stormy period, for with the assistance of a fourth engine, the steam plough smashed its way through to Winchester Junction, after which two ballast trains were hurried into the breach, and worked all night, also following day and night. On Friday, December 30th, five trains were run each way between Alton and Alresford, a very great improvement on any day's previous working. On Saturday, December 31st, five light trains were run each way between Alton and Eastleigh and continued until Tuesday, January 3rd. The ordinary service of passenger and goods trains was resumed on Wednesday, January 4th, to the great relief of all.

"The Basingstoke and Alton Light Railway had previously been cleared on January 2nd, thanks to the Engineer's Department's wonderful work in which they were ably assisted by the station-master at Basingstoke.

"As mentioned earlier in the story, the complete stoppage of all road transport threw additional work upon the rail. Meat arrived at Alton by the ton, milk traffic was doubled, passenger receipts advanced nearly £100. The station became a terminus for all trains running from Waterloo to Eastleigh, Southampton and Bournemouth *via* Alton, and the full service of trains between Alton and London was maintained throughout, which was so much appreciated by the Alton Chamber of Commerce that, upon the proposal of Mr. Boggust and carried unanimously, a hearty vote of thanks to the Southern Railway Company was passed, the Hon. Secretary writing to Waterloo as follows : "At a meeting of the Chamber of Commerce in this town, held on Monday, 2nd January, 1928, I was instructed to tender you their best thanks for the efficient way in which your Company had kept the train service, both for passengers and goods, open during the recent trying weather. - (Signed) R Vere Brown.. A unique and graceful act on the part of a body of gentlemen representing the trading interests of the town, but if you asked the stationmasters concerned what they valued most of all they would be unanimous in saying it was the kind letter of appreciation they received from the Divisional Engineer, Clapham Junction."

January 12 1928. The following letter relating to the snowstorm and the West Meon train service has been received by the General Manager: -

Sir - I am enclosing for your information a copy of a letter which appears in the current issue of *The Hampshire Chronicle.* It also gives me pleasure to endorse, so far as I know them, the facts produced by the writer. A friend of mine went to London from West Meon with relative comfort on the Tuesday afternoon. I myself went up on the Wednesday and, in spite of some damage to one of the tunnels that morning, we reached Alton rather .less than one hour late. The working of this line under very material difficulties was no doubt due very largely to the efficiency and energy of the stationmaster at West Meon and I am sure that the people of the district are grateful to him for this and for his general courtesy at all times. May I only add that the stationmaster did not ask me to write this letter and that he does not know it has been written.

Yours faithfully, H. C. W.

Bishops   Waltham.

[The letter to the *Hampshire Chronicle* referred to, corrected the statement that it was not until Wednesday afternoon that the Meon Valley route was cleared, and praised the stationmaster at West Meon, together with the engineering and operating staffs for their strenuous efforts in getting the railway clear on Tuesday].

45. - *Strawberry traffic, Wickham, 1908. Mr Foster is apparent whilst far left is Ted Hunt. One of the other men is Porter Wilsher. A horse drawn cart loaded with fruit is posed far right.*

Wickham Parish Council, Stan Woodford collection.

Strawberries and other soft fruit were long associated with the south Hampshire area and whilst it will be seen from the map the actual area was concentrated around Swanwick, various railheads, notably Botley were renowned for the despatch of soft fruit over what was a limited season. Northwards there are reports* that such traffic was heavy at both Wickham, as per the image on the previous page, and perhaps surprisingly at Mislingford siding. In addition Droxford was used for loading, possibly when congestion occurred elsewhere. The same source comments that out of season vans would be stabled at West Meon. Whilst there is no reason to totally doubt such a statement, this might seem to imply that for 46 weeks of the year vehicles would be laid up out of use, but even during the days of railway transport having a monopoly such a claim might seem slightly excessive. More like during the season, spare vehicles might be worked to West Meon and then called upon as required. As an indication of the volume of this traffic, a 1915 article in *RAILWAY & TRAVEL MONTHLY* stated that in 1914, *three million* baskets were sent from several stations by the Swanwick and District Fruit Growers Association. This does not include those sent by road to Portsmouth and Southampton nor the tons sent to the jam makers.

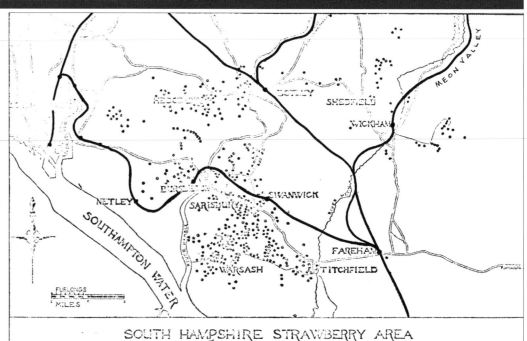

SOUTH HAMPSHIRE STRAWBERRY AREA
SHOWING DISTRIBUTION OF MEMBERS OF
THE SWANWICK & DISTRICT FRUIT GROWERS ASSOCIATION LIMITED

The same article affords some idea of the logistics involved. Prior to the season the LSWR collected some 600-700 passengers' luggage, milk, and other vacuum fitted vans and has them modified with tiers of shelves to maximise capacity. The selection of these vehicles also allows a free flow of air. "If the supply of vans runs short owing to a glut of traffic, the railway presses into service some of its old excursion stock: 14-coach set passenger trains with close buffers. The fruit is loaded on the seats, racks and floors of these carriages. Boys are employed at all the fruit-sending stations to load the fruit in the vans as they are able to crawl in-between the shelves and pack into the farthest corners". The same article gives an indication of the amount of traffic and additional staff required: Swanwick - an average of 100,000 baskets daily, two boys to each van. (A railway policeman regulates the arrival of the growers carts - pulled by donkeys, mules and horses - the queue of which can sometimes extend for one mile.) Botley handles approximately 50,000 baskets per day, this with an additional staff of about 50 during the heaviest part of the season: one foreman, six clerks, 30 porters,, and about 13 loading boys. Wickham is referred to as having three additional porters. (In the illustration, No. 45 on the previous page, 12 persons are seen. Allowing for the perhaps five regular station staff, three supernumerary, one grower with his cart, one visitor on the bicycle, and possibly the son of the station master, the figure comes close to the 12 seen. Note also in the image the familiarity of at least three of the faces with those seen at Nos. 38 and 39. The van on the extreme left may also have been 'borrowed' as it displays a distinct London & North Western Railway outline.)

From Wickham (and Mislingford) the traffic would be worked to Fareham where the MV vehicles would be added to whatever service was required, most of the strawberry trains continuing via Eastleigh to their onward destination. (The destinations were referred to by group letters from A to L. Some examples being;, Group A: North of England, Scotland and Ireland, Group B: Midlands and the North, Group C: Birmingham, Liverpool, Group E: London, Group F: GWR and South Wales destinations via Salisbury Group J: Bournemouth and south coast destinations west of Southampton, Group L: Cheltenham and other destinations on the Midland and South Western Junction Railway. etc etc.

* The South Western Circle Portfolio

STRAWBERRY TRAFFIC

A - Connect with 8 50 am from Bevois Park

B - Connect with 1 40 pm from Swanwick

C - With empty set from West Meon for Swanwick and fruit vans from Wickham, Groups C and F

D - Connect with 1 50 pm from Bevois Park. Empty set to Swanwick 3 50 p.m.

G - Van to be attached if necessary.

H - Connect with 7 45 pm Swanwick.

J - Fareham to provide Guard

K - Empty set to Swanwick on 5 15 p.m. South Wales fruit special.

Fruit from Wickham for Groups E and K to be forwarded to Fareham by the 7 32 p.m. passenger train from Alton Mondays to Fridays inclusive, and the 3 45 pm from Alton on Saturdays.

Weekdays (1919 season)								
Service No.	46		47		48		49	
No. of Engine Working	5		3 Mons. to Fri. 4. Sats.		13		12 Mons. only 13 Tues. to Fri.	
	Every weekday		Every weekday		Every weekday Sats. Excepted		Every weekday Sats. Excepted	
	ARR P.M.	DEP. P.M.	ARR P.M.	DEP. P.M.	ARR P.M.	DEP. P.M.	ARR P.M.	DEP. P.M.
Fareham	G	12 J 10		1 J 50		4 J 20		6 J 45
Wickham	12.18	12.50	1	58x	4	28	6 58	7 30
Droxford			2. 8	2.52	4 38	4 50		

Weekdays (1919 Season)										
Service No.	50		51		52		53		54	
No. of Engine Working	9		5		3 Mons. to Fri. 4 Sats		13		12 Mons. only 13 Tues. to Fris.	
To convey traffic for Group	A		B also on Sats for A		C and F				E and K	
	Every weekday Sats. excepted		Every weekday		Every weekday		Every weekday Sats. Excepted		Every weekday Sats. Excepted	
	ARR A.M.	DEP. A.M.	ARR P.M.	DEP. P.M.	ARR P.M.	DEP. P.M.	ARR P.M.	DEP. P.M.	ARR P.M.	DEP. P.M.
Droxford					2 8	2 52	4 38	4 50		
Wickham		10 0	12 13	12 J 50	3 0	3 C 15	4	58	6 53	7 30
Fareham	10 8	A	12 58	B	3 D 23	3 50	5 8	5 K 15	7 38	H
Swanwick					3 57		5 22			

A TIME FOR ECONOMY

It is a matter of regret that exact figures of expenditure against receipts have not survived for the MV railway. Even so some conclusions can be drawn even from the earliest days. Firstly there is the fact that whilst much of the civil engineering had provided for a second line of rails this was never laid. Also the train service altered little over the years, both then pointing to the conclusion that traffic did not develop in any way likely to warrant any additional investment.

Now more than a century after the line opened - and slightly more than half a century from when it closed, there is still the incorrect belief that railway closures were invariably the result of Dr Beeching. This needs to be corrected immediately. Firstly, Dr Beeching was yet to be involved with the railway industry when the Meon Valley route was closed in 1955 and secondly, and more relevantly, rationalisation, and indeed closures, of various lines in Hampshire had been taking place as far back as 1914. In that year the East Southsea and Southampton Royal Pier lines closed. The following year it was the Gosport to Stokes Bay route, none would see trains again. Three years later in 1917 it was the Basingstoke to Alton line (this would re-open in 1924). There was then a hiatus until the 1930s, but in 1931 it was the turn of the Hurstbourne to Fullerton, and Lee-on-the-Solent routes. The next year 1932 the re-opened Basingstoke to Alton line closed again and there would be no second reprieve. The Bishops Waltham branch followed in 1933 and finally in Hampshire the Ringwood to Christchurch route succumbed in 1935. Some of these would survive for many years in whole or part for freight, whilst in addition there were closures of stations on existing lines, economies at existing stations similar to those applied at Privett (described below) as well as similar closure elsewhere on the Southern system. Elsewhere technology would allow signalling to be centralised and rationalisation applied - ie at Butts Junction.

Locally we cannot be certain if closure was a considered factor for the MV during either LSWR or SR ownership, possibly the strategic importance of the line as a means of transportation to the naval ports outweighed closure plans, especially in the 1930s, but it must be noted that just 19 years after opening economy was undertaken both from an infrastructure and personnel perspective. Commencing first at Privett, with effect from 20 June 1922, the passing loop was de-commissioned but retained as a shunting loop. The signalling here was also removed, the revised tablet section now from Tisted to West Meon, a distance of seven miles. From a practical perspective with the exception of Farringdon Goods, it was only at the southern end stations, West Meon, Droxford and Wickham that traffic was in any way sufficient to warrant the retention of facilities, Tisted might equally easily have succumbed had it not been for fact this would have created an even longer 12 mile section from Butts Junction south. It is clear from an operational perspective it would be either Tisted or Privett where the axe would fall, the latter being selected.

With only one platform in use at Privett the footbridge was therefore redundant and would have been removed at the same time. All the footbridges at the other stations were of timber construction and likely to have been in need of substantive repair after 20+ years, these too then succumbed (West Meon around October 1922 - see below). Certainly all had gone by the mid 1930s with that at Wickham possibly the last to go.

In the same year, 1922, 'Signal Instruction No. 12' gave details of an alteration in the placing of the Down Starting Signal at West Meon. "To be carried out on Thursday 19 October. The down starting signal will be refixed about 40 yards nearer the station. The work will be in progress from 10.0 am until completed. Mr. Partridge to provide flagman, as required." This came about in consequence of a break being made in the platforms at the south end near to the signal box and a new board crossing provided: this work would have been consistent with the removal of the footbridge here. Passengers would now cross the line under the immediate eye of the signalman. At the same time

46. - An undated view of West Meon looking south from the usual vantage point. What the photographer has captured is an image taken very soon after the removal of the footbridge and shortening of the platforms - indicated. The date may be guessed at as between October 1922 and no later than about 1925.

as the re-siting of the down starting signal occurred, the water column at the end of the down platform was also re-positioned to the end of the shortened platform. Little if any use was found for the now isolated shortened platforms at the south end.

The goods sheds were next. Dates for removal are not completely clear but this may have been as maintenance was necessary or in an effort to reduce the rateable value of the fixed assets. Those at Farringdon and Wickham remained until the end, neither documentary nor photographic evidence is available to support removal dates elsewhere. (It may be reasonable to assume that at Privett at least the goods shed was removed in 1922 - the 5 ton yard crane from Privett had certainly been removed by 1935.) One goods shed also found a new use, being dismantled and re-erected at Fawley, when this new branch line opened in 1925.

Finally we come to the staff numbers which, as can be seen commenced with a downgrading from that of a station master post to a 'Porter in Charge'. Again it was the stations which conducted the most

LONDON & SOUTH WESTERN RAILWAY. Instruction No. 7. 1922.

Instructions to all concerned as to the
ABOLITION OF PRIVETT AS A TABLET SECTION AND NEW AND ALTERED SIGNALS, ETC.

ABOLITION OF PRIVETT SIGNAL BOX AS A TABLET SECTION.

After the arrival of the 8.5 p.m. train from Fareham at Tisted on Monday, 19th June, the signal box at Privett Station will be abolished as a tablet section, and the section will in future be as between Tisted and West Meon, the first train to pass through the new section being the 4.50 a.m. from Waterloo on Tuesday, 20th June. The signal box will be converted into a ground frame box.

On completion of the work, all trains will run over the down loop at Privett, the existing up loop being used as a siding, with facing points in the running line at each end of the station. These points, together with those giving access to the down sidings, will be operated from the ground frame box and controlled by the tablet for the Tisted—West Meon section, in accordance with the regulations for controlling sidings by means of the electric train tablet.

A new connection, which will be facing for down trains, has been provided at the West Meon end of the station, giving access to the down siding.

Catch points have been provided in the up siding (existing up loop) at the Tisted end of the station.

Lamps, shewing amber lights, have been fixed to the posts which hitherto carried the down and up distant signals, for the purpose of enabling enginemen to readily locate their position when approaching the station.

The following will be removed :—
The down and up distant signal arms.
The down and up home and starting signals.
The points in the existing up loop leading to the down siding.
The catch points in the up siding.
The ground signals controlling the following movements :—
From the existing up loop to the down or up sidings.
From the up siding to the existing up loop.
From the down sidings to the down loop.
From the down siding to the existing up loop.
From the down loop to the down sidings.

The work will be commenced after the arrival of the 8.5 p.m. train from Fareham at Tisted, on Monday, 19th June.
Mr. Delia to provide flagmen as required.

(W. 167.)

47. - High summer at Privett. Edward Griffith's classic pose in early British Railways days, 24 June 1949, of 'L12' No. No. 30420 northbound on the former down line at Privett. The grass-grown former up platform is on the right. With just five revenue earning vehicles in tow - and a distinctly empty looking yard, there was clearly little revenue to be generated here. Discussion on the removal of the loop and closure of the signal box has begun at Waterloo in 1920, some two years before action was actually taken.

48. - *Later on in years at West Meon, showing the shortened platform and board crossing - the down starting signal and water column are just out of sight to the right. The rear of various notices 'STOP-LOOK-LISTEN' and 'Not to Trespass' can also be seen. With no need for maintenance the unused portions of platform have also succumbed to nature. The physical placement of the station buildings and signal boxes at the other stations meant there was no justification in foreshortening the platforms elsewhere.*

SOUTHERN RAILWAY.

Signal Instruction No. 5, 1935.

Instructions to all concerned as to
CONVERSION OF EXISTING DOWN AND UP LINES BETWEEN ALTON AND BUTTS JUNCTION INTO SINGLE LINES; ABOLITION OF BUTTS JUNCTION SIGNAL BOX

and

NEW AND ALTERED SIGNALS, Etc.

Rules 77, 78, 79 and 80 to be observed. Drivers to keep a good look-out for hand signals.

BUTTS JUNCTION AND ALTON.

To be carried out on Sunday, 17th February, commencing at 12.5 a.m.

BUTTS JUNCTION BOX.

Butts Junction signal box and all signals and points (except those leading to Treloar Cripples Home Siding) will be abolished. The tablet instruments will be transferred to Alton signal box and the sections will then be Alton-Tisted and Alton-Medstead respectively.

The existing down line as between Alton and Butts Junction will, in future, be worked as a single line for Meon Valley line trains.

The existing up line as between Butts Junction and Alton will, in future, be worked as a single line for Mid Hants line trains.

A new two-lever ground frame, controlled by the tablet for the Alton—Medstead section, will be provided near the existing Butts Junction signal box, for operating the points leading to Treloar Cripples Home Siding. The existing double catch points in this siding will be abolished and new catch points will be provided at the clearance point of the connection with the Mid Hants line. The siding will, in future, be worked by special services from Alton. Vehicles will be hauled from Alton with a brake van at the rear and propelled from the siding to Alton with the brake van leading; the loads of goods trains must be limited to 20 wagons.

business that retained the senior post the longest. Tisted and Privett had been downgraded by 1922/23, with Droxford and it is believed Wickham a few years afterwards. The post would remain at West Meon with the incumbent there taking charge of the other stations. Again this was a common practice. (The station master post at Wickham was reinstated later).

The final change to affect the line was in 1935 when Butts Junction Signal Box was abolished. From that time on instead of a physical junction at the latter location, the route was run as two parallel single lines with the tablet section extended to be from Tisted to Alton. Necessary alternations to the signalling at Alton were concurrently undertaken.

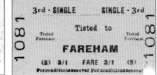

Opposite page - Working timetable 1 June to 30 September 1909.

Services on the Meon Valley line commenced with six trains each way on weekdays (as Saturday was at the time a working day, and would continue to be so for some years, this too was considered a weekday) and two each way on Sundays. Passenger timings were leisurely, one hour - give or take a minute, between Fareham and Alton inclusive of five stops. Deducting 'station time' at each, eight minutes, and this gives a start to stop average of 30 mph. Allowing for the necessary starting and stopping and it is likely speeds of 50 mph were regularly attained. By 1906 what is interesting is that already two minutes station time was allowed at West Meon, Droxford, and Wickham, but only one minute at Tisted and Privett, an early reflection of the limited traffic at these locations. Even so it appears there was some attempt by Waterloo to promote the railway as a through route, for apart from any special workings, examples of which are referred to later, two of the weekday services were through trains to Gosport, a practice that would become more common in later year. More pointed was that one working in each direction started and terminated at Waterloo, albeit even if the journey time north of Alton was at the same leisurely pace as applied on the Meon Valley line itself. Two passenger services ran on Sundays, both through services between Alton and Portsmouth. Passengers for London having to change trains at Alton.

Weekdays, two goods services plied their own leisurely way over the line calling at every station as well as at the sidings at Farringdon and Mislingford. Both sidings were shown as being called at regardless as to whether it was an Up goods (Fareham to Alton) or Down working, but without the facility of a run-round loop at either, no doubt at certain times recourse was probably made to hand or fly-shunting. Of course, that is not say there would be traffic to collect or deliver from every location every day, but to cater for eventualities the timetable allowed for between 10 and 36 minutes to be spent at the various locations. As might be expected, the shorter timescale was applicable to the two northernmost stations. Freight services took around three hours to travel the line between Alton and Fareham. At this point it may be appropriate to pause for a moment to consider the type of traffic that would have been received or despatched over the line. In reality, and certainly before competition from road, this would have been everything needed by the local populace, or produced locally and destined for market. Harvest time and winter time (coal) would have witnessed increased volumes. Thus in the former category the local station master would telegraph his requirements to Southampton (the Meon Valley line came under the LSWR Central District) and an empty wagon would be delivered the next day ready to be loaded. In the reverse direction a full wagon of produce would arrive and be left for unloading. The consignee was permitted a certain length of time to complete

1st JUNE to 30th SEPTEMBER, 1909, or until further notice. 125

MEON VALLEY (ALTON AND FAREHAM) LINE.

FOR SPEED RESTRICTIONS SEE PAGES A, B, C, D, E, F & G.

This is a Single Line from Butts Junction to Fareham Junction and is worked under the Regulations for working Single Lines by the Electric Train Tablet Block System.

unloading, otherwise a demurrage charge, basically a rental for the actual wagon and siding space occupied, would be applied. This could sometimes cause friction between the station master and customer. Small loads might similarly be collected / delivered to the station by the customer, or recourse made to a local carrier. There is no indication who the various carriers might have been to undertake this service, but it may well have been that a local individual undertook this service - see image 7 in Book 1. Regretfully neither in early or later timetables is there any indication that the Meon Valley was ever used as a regular through route for freight. As will have been gathered, predicting freight patterns was not easy. In practical terms the goods working did not always ashere to the booked times at each station. No doubt with local knowledge that there was little work at one location on a particular day but more than usual at another, local arrangements would be made to run early or make up time later. Even so care had to be taken not to miss a booked crossing or delay a passenger working. The maximum loading for freight trains, and again dependent upon the power of the locomotive used, was 40 wagons.

By 1914 some minor alterations had been made to the Sunday service, in that both Up trains were shown as through workings to Waterloo even if one only ran as far as Aldershot where passengers were faced with a 50 minute wait. In the down direction the 6.10 pm divided at Aldershot, one portion destined for Southampton via the Mid Hants line and the other over the Meon Valley to Portsmouth. Some advertised through workings would continue until 1937. At this time electrification reached Alton - it would never venture further. The Meon Valley thus became a shuttle service although the Mid Hants would continue to see some regular Southampton - Waterloo workings for many years to come (the latter excluding the various diversions which became commonplace especially in the mid 1960s).

Also pre WW1, an interesting 'half service' was the Saturday 9.40 pm from Gosport which ran north but only as far as West Meon. This would benefit anyone returning after an evening out in Fareham (not sure the term 'revellers' would really apply to passengers to the Meon Valley). After arrival at West Meon the engine would run-round and the service returned south as a public working at 10.30 pm. In reality it was unlikely there would have been many takers at this late hour. Another slightly strange working was the Sunday morning 7.25 am from Portsmouth, destined for Wickham. Here after a sojourn of just 15 minutes it returned. What the intended passenger traffic was can only be guessed at: certainly the time was too short for religious observance. Even so it continued to appear in the timetable for some years, but altered as starting and finishing at Fareham and now with a one hour wait at Wickham.

During LSWR days, coaching stock was usually a standard 4-coach set of non-corridor stock which afforded plenty of room. One working however, the 10.41 am north from Fareham, was shown as formed of two such sets. This may have been because this was a through Waterloo working or simply a means of returning vehicles to where they would commence their next booked diagram.

Unlike some other railways, the LSWR regularly formed much of their coaching stock into 'sets' - a practice that would continue with the Southern Railway and later still under the Southern Region of British Railways. Accordingly there were also 3-coach sets, and these too would be seen on some Meon Valley services. To cater for increased demand on Saturdays, additional vehicles, normally separate 3rd class accommodation, would be added as required. Mixed trains, meaning passenger and freight as were run on certain routes, were not permitted on the line.

The LSWR and later the SR and BR(S) would produce weekly notices indicating alterations to regular timetabled services as well as additional trains and also cancellations. Some of these have survived from the 1914 period and make for interesting reading. The first is a special train for a Musical Ride Party from Portsmouth to Aldershot on Sunday 14 June shown as under. Interestingly no return working is indicated.

No. 13.—Musical Ride Party, Portsmouth to Aldershot.—2 officers, 36 men, 6 guns and limbers, 46 horses in trucks.

A special train will run as under :—

	ARR. A.M.	DEP. A.M.
Portsmouth Tn.	...	10 0
Fratton	10 4	
Portcreek Jct.	10 10	
Cosham Jct.	10 12	
Fareham	10 25*	
Wickham	10 34*	
Droxford	10 42*	
West Meon	10 49*	
Privett	10 × 58	11 9
Tisted	11 16*	
Butts Jct.	11 23*	
Aldershot	**1148**	...

Fratton Loco. to provide engine.

Portsmouth to provide train complete.

Inspector Kirk, guard.   (N. 41,573.)

(An 'X' in the timings indicates where the special train would cross another service.)

Another special working in the following month was a Sunday school outing. In this particular case the two extra vehicles - a bit cramped surely with 200 adults and children in just two coaches - would have been worked to Alton and then possibly detached, ready to return south later in the day. On the same

On WEDNESDAY, 15th July.

No. 101.—Congregational S.S.—About 200 adults and children will leave Gosport for Wickham by the 1.0 p.m. train, returning at 7.48 p.m.

Gosport to attach 2 extra thirds to the 1.0 p.m. thence and reserve for the party. The vehicles to go through as under :—

To reserve	class accommodation.					
	P.M.	P.M.			P.M.	P.M.
Gosport	...	1 0		Alton	...	7 6
Fareham	1 11	1 37		Wickham	...	7 48
Wickham	1 45	...		Fareham	7 56	8 5
Alton	**2 28**	...		**Gosport**	**8 16**	...

Stations concerned to arrange transfer.   (N. 41,724.) (B. 1/210,803.)

MEON VALLEY LINE.

Left half

	WEEK DAYS.									SUNDAYS.		
	a.m.	a.m.	a.m.	p.m.	p.m.	p.m.	p.m.	p.m.		a.m.	a.m.	p.m.
LONDON (W'loo) dep.	7 10	9 25	940	1T 5	1s10	4 12	530		...	850	610	
Woking .... ,,	7 47	10 10	1045	2T 12	s 0	4 51	6 6		...	9 50	6 51	
Aldershot .... ,,	8 18	10 35	1115	2T33	2s32	5 16	6 32		...	1017	7 50	
Farnham .... ,,	8 27	10 43	1124	2T43	2s43	5 24	6 41		...	1026	7 59	
Bentley .... ,,	8 37	10 53	1135	2T53	2s53	5 33	6 50		...	1035	8 8	
ALTON .... arr.	845	11 1	1143	3T 1	3s 15	5 41	658		...	1044	816	
ALTON .... dep.	857	11 12	1155	**3 9**		5 46	7 6		...	1050	820	
Tisted (for Selborne) arr.	9 7	11 22	12 5	3 19		5 56	7 16		...	1059	8 29	
Privett .... ,,	9 14	11 32	1212	3 26		6 3	7 23		...	11 6	8 36	
West Meon .... ,,	9 21	11 39	1219	3 33		6 10	7 31	10†30	...	1113	843	
Droxf'd (for H'bledon),,	9 29	11 46	1226	3 40		6 17	7 39	10 56	...	1120	8 50	
Wickham .... ,,	9 37	11 57	1234	3 48		6 25	7 47	10 44	8†40	1128	8 58	
Knowle Platform ... ,,	9 43	...	1239	**N**			**P**					
Fareham .... ,,	9 48	12 6	1244	3 57		6 34	7 56	10 53	8 48	1137	9 7	
Fareham .... dep.	10 5	12 25	1 15	4 10		6 43	5 11	51054	1143	9 40		
Fort Brockhurst arr.	1012	12 31	1 21	4 17		6 49	12 11	12 11 0	1149	9 46		
GOSPORT ... * ,,	1016	12 35	1 25	4 21		6 53	816	11 16	11 4	1153	950	
Gosport Road ... ,,	1022	...	2 15	5 9								
Stokes Bay .... ,,	1026	...	2 19	5 13								
Fareham .... dep.	9 54	12K16	1 6	4 8		6 50	8 29	10 59	8 52	1140	9 10	
Portchester .... ,,	10 0	12K23		4 15		6 57	...	11 6	8 59	1147	9 17	
Cosham .... ,,	10 6	12K31	1 17	4 24		7 3	8 39	11 13	9 5	1155	9 23	
Fratton & Southsea arr.	1014	12K39	1 25	4 32		7 11	8 47	11 21	9 13	12 3	9 3	
PORTSMOUTH TOWN ,,	1018	12K44	1 30	4 37		7 15	8 52	11 25	9 17	12 7	936	

Right half

	WEEK DAYS.									SUNDAYS.		
	a.m.	a.m.	p.m.	p.m.	p.m.	p.m.	p.m.	p.m.	a.m.	a.m.	p.m.	
PORTSMOUTH T'N dep.	7 3	9 50	12H42	1 J0	3 40	527	6 53	9 15	725	7 55	6 50	
Fratton & Southsea ,,	7 7	9 55	12H47	1 J5	3 45	5 31	7 3	9 20	7 29	7 58	6 55	
Cosham .... ,,	7 16	10 5	12H57	1 J14	3 55	...	7 13	9 29	7 38	8 8	7 4	
Portchester .... ,,	7 22	1012	1H 4	1 J21	4 2	...	7 20	9 36	...	8 15	7 10	
Fareham .... arr.	7 28	1018	1H10	1 J27	4 8	5 47	7 26	9 42	7 47	8 21	7 16	
Stokes Bay ...) dep.	...	9 30	11H55	11 55	2 27	4 28	6 55	...	...	...	...	
Gosport Road	,,	...	9 34	11H59	11J59	2 31	4 32	6 59	...	...	...	...
GOSPORT * ,,	715	10 5	1H 0	1 J03	43 4	57	7 8	9 40	...	8 10	7 3	
F't Brockhurst ,,	7 19	10 9	1H 4	1 J43	47 5	1	7 12	9 44	...	8 14	7 7	
Fareham .... arr.	7 25	1015	1H11	1 J11	3 54	5 8	7 19	9 50	...	8 20	7 13	
Fareham .... dep.	7 30	1041		1 37	4 30	5 55	7 35	9 52	7 48	8 30	7 20	
Knowle Platform ... ,,		1046		**RQ**			7 40	9 57			7 26	
Wickham .... ,,	7 39	1051		1 46	4 39	6 4	7 49	10 2	7f56	8 39	7 32	
Dr'f d (for H'mbledn),,	7 50	11 1		1 56	4 49	6 19	8 0	10 12		8 49	7 41	
West Meon .... ,,	7 59	11 9		2 4	4 58	6 27	8 8	10f19	stop	8 57	7 54	
Privett .... ,,	8 9	1119		2 14	5 8	6 37	8 18		...	9 7	8 5	
Tisted (for Selborne) ,,	8 15	1125		2 20	5 14	6 43	8 24		...	9 13	8 12	
ALTON .... arr.	823	1133		2 28	5 22	6 51	832		...	9 21	820	
ALTON .... dep.	839	1138		2 31	5 35	659	835		...	9 24	825	
Bentley .... arr.	8 47	1146		2 39	5 41	7 7	8 43		...	9 32	8 33	
Farnham .... ,,	8 56	1154		2 47	5 50	7 15	8 51		...	9 40	8 42	
Aldershot .... ,,	9 6	12 4		2 56	5 59	7 24	8 59		...	9 49	8 52	
Woking .... ,,	9 33	12L54		3 21	6 25	7 48	9L55		...	1052	9 18	
LONDON (W'loo) ,,	1013	1 3		4 13	7 6	848	10L55		...	1146	10 7	

* For complete Service of Trains between Fareham, Gosport, Gosport Road and Stokes Bay, see other pages. K First and Third Classes only. N Stops at Knowle Platform on Thursdays to take up or set down passengers. P Stops at Knowle Platform on Saturdays to take up or set down passengers. S Saturdays only. T Saturdays excepted. † Depart.

* For complete Service of Trains between Stokes Bay, Gosport Road, Gosport and Fareham, see other pages. H Commencing 1st July. J June only. L Change at Aldershot. f Arrive. Q Stops at Knowle platform on the 1st Wednesday in each Month to take up or set down passengers. R Stops at Knowle Platform on Thursdays to take up or set down passengers.

---

day there was a excursion to Portsmouth with the following timings.

On WEDNESDAY, 15th July.

20

MR. HUNT'S EXCURSIONS TO PORTSMOUTH.

Special trains will run as under :—

No. 120.

North Camp	ARR. A.M.	DEP. A.M.
North Camp	...	**6 0**
Butts Junc. ...		6 45*
Tisted ...	6 52	6 53
Privett ...	6 59	7 0
West Meon...	7 6	7 7
Droxford ...	7 13	7 14
Wickham ...	7 21	7 22
Fareham ...		7 30*A
Cosham Junc. ...		7 42
Portcreek Junc. ...		7 44
Fratton ...	7 59	8 1
Portsmouth Tn.	8 4	

A—Precede 6.40 a.m. from Southampton.

No. 121.

	ARR. P.M.	DEP. P.M.
Portsmouth Tn.		**8 30**
Fratton ...	8 32	8 33
Portcreek Junc. ...		8 38
Cosham Junc. ...		8 40
Fareham ...		8 51*
Wickham ...	9 0	9 2
Droxford ...	9 12	9 14
West Meon ...	9 22	9 23
Privett ...	9 33	9 34
Tisted ...	9 39	9 40
Butts Junc. ...		9 47*
North Camp	**10 27**	...

An * in this and other notices indicated where a train might not stop but it was necessary to collect / deposit the single line tablet.

Another day when two specials were run on to and off the line was 29 June. From the north this was train No. 130, run for the 'Childrens Holiday Fund.' Again no return working is indicated. The temptation is to suggest the party may have returned by service train, but if a special were required for the outward working it is doubtful if sufficient accommodation could have been provided without at least strengthening a regular service - as had been the case with the earlier Sunday School outing of 15 July. Unfortunately in all these examples the formation of the train is not given.

No. 130.

	ARR. P.M.	DEP. P.M.
Waterloo	...	**12 8**
Butts Junc. ...		2 10*
Tisted ...	2 18	2 x 21
Privett ...	2 27	2 29
West Meon ...	2 35	2 38
Droxford	**2 44**	...
Central.		

D—Engine to run light to Eastleigh unless otherwise ordered.

(N. 41,800).

No. 131.

	ARR. P.M.	DEP. P.M.
Droxford ...	2 44	2 50
Wickham ...		2 57*
Fareham ...	3 † 5	D

The second special of 29 June was a private party from Waterloo to what is intriguingly referred to as 'Alton (New Platform)' - a repeat with the same destination / designation was made in September 1914. Although the destination is not Meon valley related, clearly it was necessary to work the stock for stabling at Tisted after which the engine ran light to Aldershot before it (or more likely another locomotive) ran back to fetch the stock ready to collect the party again at Alton. What is intriguing is the reference to the Alton destination. There was no 'new' platform at Alton, although it had been in 1902 when the former down platform was extended into an island. Possibly this is the answer, the destination was the new (recent) side to the island platform but still referred to by the railway as 'new'.

On MONDAY, 29th June.

5

PRIVATE PARTY, WATERLOO TO ALTON (NEW PLATFORM) AND BACK.

Special train will run as under :—

No. 14.	ARR. P.M.	DEP. P.M.		No. 15.	ARR. P.M.	DEP. P.M.
Alton New Platform	...	2†27		Tisted ...	4 ‖ 20	4†50
				Butts Junction	4 57	5 6
Butts Junction	2 29	2 30		*Alton New Platform*		
Tisted ...	2†37	2 ‖ 50		...	5 † 8	...

ENGINE WORKING.

No. 16.	ARR. P.M.	DEP. P.M.		No. 17.	ARR. P.M.	DEP. P.M.
Tisted ...	2†37	2‖50	(N. 41,291.)	*Aldershot* ...	...	3 ‖ 40
Butts Junction		2 57*		Butts Junction		4‖13*
Aldershot ...	3 ‖ 21	...		Tisted ...	4 ‖ 20	4†50

No. 18.—For particulars of Season Excursions see Season Excursion Notice No. 804.

The final workings that may be referred to are two special trains to the Cattle Sale at Wickham. Both are from 1914 although the first cannot be ascribed to a particular date. Apart from the dates the workings of both are identical and are what would later be referred to as 'Q' paths, meaning they would run if required. Again there is intrigue for although these are shown as special workings *from* Wickham, how did the cattle get *to* Wickham? Unless said beasts had been walked in from various farms or brought in sporadically by the local goods service over the preceding days. (Such would be an example of a station master telegraphing for a cattle wagon to be brought to him ready for loading.) The issue of cheap-day return tickets is also of interest, the reason

CATTLE SALE AT WICKHAM.

No. 125.—Cheap third class return tickets to be issued to **Wickham** from Tisted, Cosham, Gosport, Bishops Waltham, Fareham and certain intermediate stations.

For full particulars see public bill. (B. 209,742.)

If required an engine, van and guard will leave Fareham at 6.15 p.m. for Wickham, returning at 7.10 p.m. with cattle as under :—

No. 126.	ARR. P.M.	DEP. P.M.		
Fareham ...	...	6 A 15	A—Engine, van and guard. B—With cattle.
Wickham ...	6 A 24	...	The Fareham shunting engine to work this service.
Wickham ...	...	7 B 10	Fareham to arrange and provide van and guard.
Fareham ...	7 B 20	...	

Traffic for Portsmouth and L. B. & S. C. Railway **must be forwarded from** Fareham by the 6.50 p.m. Goods from Eastleigh. (N. 40,518.)

Central.

for the inclusion of Bishops Waltham being that by road the town was only 4½ miles distant - much further by rail with a circular journey to Botley, Fareham and then back to Wickham. It likely that potential purchasers / spectators may have been from the Bishops Waltham catchment area.

On THURSDAY, 17th September.

CATTLE SALE AT WICKHAM.

No. 14.—Cheap third class return tickets to be issued to **Wickham** from Tisted, Cosham, Gosport, Bishops Waltham, Fareham and certain intermediate stations.

For full particulars see public bill.

If required an engine, van and guard will leave Fareham at 6.15 p.m. for Wickham, returning at 7.10 p.m. with cattle as under :—

No. 15.	ARR. P.M.	DEP. P.M.		
Fareham ...	...	6 A 15	A—Engine, van and guard. B—With cattle.
Wickham ...	6 A 24	...	The Fareham shunting engine to work this service.
Wickham ...	...	7 B 10	Fareham to arrange and provide van and guard.
Fareham ...	7 B 20	...	

Traffic for Portsmouth and L. B. & S. C. Railway **must be forwarded from** Fareham by the 6.50 p.m. Goods from Eastleigh. (N. 40,530.)

One final special working known to have taken place, but not located in the notices, were trains for race-goers to Droxford and invariably from London. These may also have been the only occasion (apart from Mr Churchill's train in 1944 when a restaurant car may have been seen on the line. Details of any such special working are not known but they did continued sometime into WW1 as Droxford races became more popular following the temporary closure of several of the London courses then used as military compounds.

For many years the general timetables were issued twice yearly, that for the summer running for a shorter period than the remainder of the year. Supplements, in the form of the weekly 'Special Traffic Notices' previously described, and for particular events / occasions were also issued. At the start of each of the main issues there was also a list of changes to existing services. Some of these might be relatively minor - a minute or two alteration in an arrival or departure time, but also cancellations and new workings. One affecting the summer service for 1914 relates to an item already discussed. "7.48 am Fareham to West Meon (7.25 from Portsmouth) will not run beyond Wickham." The corresponding down working was also cancelled as under, "8.24 am West Meon to Portsmouth discontinued as between West Meon and Wickham. Start from Wickham at 8.24 am. This train calls at Knowle Platform on receipt by the station master at Wickham or of a request from Dr Abbott or the Clerk to the Asylum." For many years visiting day at Knowle was Thursday and so again the Wickham station master was responsible for advising the driver to stop at Knowle if necessary. (A persistent rumour has it that a director of the LSWR had to be transported to Knowle as a patient. His name or fate are not recorded save that a special train was used.) Again this may be seen as an indication that even though it was the southern end of the line that generated the most business, this was primarily from Wickham.

At the start of WW1 it was very much a question of business as usual for the Meon Valley. What was apparent was that the LSWR immediately issued a system-wide notice that until further notice various types of goods would not be handled. A number of goods services were also cancelled on a several lines although with only two goods trains daily it would have been difficult to make cuts on the MV. The general reduction was to allow greater capacity for military traffic. As time passed so these restrictions eased although shortage of manpower would lead to a reduction to four trains each way by 1918. The Sunday service had also been withdrawn. (Probably as with elsewhere there were now women working at one or more of the stations on the line but this cannot be confirmed.)

Post 1918 services gradually returned to pre-war levels although increasing costs, wages and coal primarily, resulted in a long hard look at existing resources, hence the economy effected at Privett in 1922.

LONDON, ALTON, DROXFORD, FAREHAM, EASTLEIGH, and SOUTHAMPTON.

Right timetable — June / July 1934

Above - 'Bradshaws', July 1919. Right - June / July 1934.

ALTON, WEST MEON, and FAREHAM.—London and South Western.

Post WW1, gradually the service of six passenger trains way weekdays, the two Sunday trains plus the each way goods on weekdays were restored. This pattern continued until about 1936 although at some stage the early morning Sunday train to Wickham had disappeared whilst passenger timings were generally about 5-10 minutes slower than they had been pre-war. One fact about the 1930s was that the timings were also better spread throughout the day, rather than having uneven long gaps between trains. There was also some additional business with the opening of a passenger halt at Farringdon in May 1931, although a petition for a similar facility and goods siding at Meonstoke, between Droxford and West Meon was not proceeded with. 1936 was also the final year of the through Waterloo services, whilst 1937 may well have been the time when two-coach push-pull passenger workings became the norm during the day, although it was noted that the first and last trains on weekdays were loco hauled. The Sunday service had also increased to three trains each way. All of these ran through to Portsmouth (for Southsea) and were reportedly well filled with trippers. (We do not know if at this time the Sunday service was loco-hauled or push-pull, presumably the former if the loading is to be believed. Even so, a two-coach push-pull set was a poor substitute for a four-coach set in pre WW1 days.) The freight service in 1939 was still ran each way daily including on Saturday.

Later and in the immediate post WW2 period revenue was not quite as bad as has been believed in the past. This is judged by the fact that no reduction in service took place until 1951 when the daily count was slashed to just four

LONDON, ALTON, DROXFORD, FAREHAM, EASTLEIGH, and SOUTHAMPTON.

(Detailed public timetable — Down and Up trains, Week Days and Sundays)

Down stations include: London (Waterloo) 192, Alton, Farringdon, Tisted, Privett, West Meon, Droxford, Wickham, Knowle Platform, Fareham 184, 187, Fort Brockhurst, Gosport, Alton, Medstead, Ropley, Alresford, Itchen Abbas, Winchester, Shawford, Eastleigh 184, 187, Swaythling, St. Denys 184, Northam, Southampton.

Up stations include: Southampton Ter., Northam, St. Denys, Swaythling, Eastleigh, Shawford, Winchester, Itchen Abbas, Alresford, Ropley, Medstead, Alton 193, Gosport, Fort Brockhurst, Fareham, Wickham, Knowle Platform, Droxford, West Meon, Privett, Tisted, Alresford, Farringdon, Alton 193, London (Waterloo) 193.

Footnotes:
A Station for Selborne (4½ miles). B Station for Hambledon (3¼ miles). C 1 mile from Cheesehill Station. D Sta. for Twyford, d 4 mins. later on Sats. F Station for Bishopstoke. G Southampton Terminus, for Docks. H Thro Train, Deal, Dover, and Folkestone to Bournemouth, see pages 330a, 292, 290, 192, & 156a. H Dep. 6 27 aft. Sats. h Thro Train, Aldershot to Portsmouth and Southsea, pages 192a and 189a. ƒ Dep. 4 21 aft. Sats. SX Sats. excepted. ∫ Southampton Central. Q Thro Train, Bournemouth West to Folkestone, Dover, & Deal, via Guildford, pages 159a, 193, 292, 290, & 329. ‡ Dep. 7 27 mrn. on Sats. † 7 mins. earlier Sats. y Thro Train, Portsmouth and Southsea to Aldershot, pages 189 and 192a. ¶ 6 mins. later on Sats. ‡ Arr. 2 10 aft. Sats. LOCAL TRAINS between Winchester and Southampton, page 184—Fareham and Gosport, 184.

OTHER TRAINS between London and Southampton, page 154—Knowle Platform and Fareham, 184.

Left - Public timetable, 4 July to 26 September 1937.

Bottom, 49. - Watched by an admiring audience, 'M7' No. 54 pauses at Privett, en-route to Alton.

Opposite page, top left, 50. - 'M7' No. 30480 nearing Privett with a push-pull working sometime between 1948 and 1955. Where once four coaches and often a van had been necessary, now there were just two.

Opposite page, bottom left, 51.– Tisted, 7.30 pm, Sunday 1 June 1947. The train is the 6.07 pm from Portsmouth, due at Alton at 7.37½ pm. Two up passenger trains used the line on a Sunday at this time, this service and one other two hours later.

Opposite page, right, 52. - The companion view to that at No. 47. 'L12' No. 30420 , this time near West Meon.

---

trains each way and the Sunday workings withdrawn. Weekdays the locals now referred to the trains as the 'Breakfast time' train, the 'Lunch-time' train, 'Tea-time train' etc. The Saturday freight service succumbed in 1952 after which this reduced pattern of four trains each way, plus a daily freight Monday to Friday remained until closure.

As with pre WW2, the line was used for the occasional excursion right up to closure. Children from the MV travelling to school at Fareham was one form of regular traffic as were children travelling daily in the reverse direction to the Westbury School at West Meon. Neither, however would be sufficient to prevent closure.

Non-revenue earning trains also appeared as necessary over the years. These would be various types of engineer's workings necessary for maintenance, whilst further down the scale a wagon of sleepers might also be delivered via the daily goods service into a yard nearest the site of work. Other staff, the signal lineman for example, might travel by service train to the necessary area needing his attention.

Table 71 LONDON, ALTON, DROXFORD, FAREHAM, EASTLEIGH, and SOUTHAMPTON

Miles	Down	Week Days															Sundays					
		a.m	a.m.	a.m	a.m	a.m	a.m	a.m	p.m	p.m	p.m	p.m	p.m	p.m	p.m	p.m	a.m	a.m		p.m	p.m	
	Waterloo 76 dep	5 55	6 25	7 25	7 28	7y25	10y27	11z57	12z57	2y27	2z57	3y27	4K47	5 57	5 57	6 57	7 25	1027	..	3 27	6 57	..
46½	Alton dep.	7 38	..	Saturdays excepted	Saturdays only	9 5	..	1 30	..	..	4 30	..	..	Saturdays excepted	Saturdays only	..	..	..	..	..	..	..
50½	Farringdon	7 45	..			9 12	..	1 37	..	..	4 37	..	..			..	..	..	..	..	..	..
52¼	Tisted	7 50	..			9 16	..	1 41	..	..	4 41	..	..			..	..	..	..	..	..	..
55¾	Privett	7 57	..			9 24	..	1 49	..	..	4 48	..	..			..	..	..	..	..	..	..
59½	West Meon	8 5	..			9 31	..	1 56	..	..	4 56	..	..			..	..	..	..	..	..	..
63¾	Droxford B	8 15	..			9 39	..	2 4	..	..	5 3	..	..			..	..	..	..	..	..	..
68¼	Wickham	8 27	..			9 48	..	2 13	..	..	5 12	..	..			..	..	..	..	..	..	..
70½	Knowle Halt	8 32	..			9 54	..	2 19	..	..	5 18	..	..			..	..	..	..	..	..	..
72¾	Fareham arr.	8 37	..			9 59	..	2 24	..	..	5 23	..	..			..	..	..	..	..	..	..
76½	Fort Brockhurst	..	..			1023	..	..	..	..	6 24	..	..			..	..	..	..	..	..	..
77¾	Gosport arr.	..	..			1027	..	..	..	..	6 28	..	..			..	..	..	..	..	..	..
—	Alton dep.	..	7 53	8 55	9 15	..	12 5	..	2 30	4 10	..	5 5	6 2	7 25	7 30	8 38	9 0	12 5	..	4 55	8 20	..
51½	Medstead & Four Marks	..	8 5	9 7	9 27	..	12 17	..	2 42	4 22	..	5 17	6 14	7 37	7 42	8 50	9 12	1217	..	5 7	8 32	..
54½	Ropley	..	8 11	9 12	9 33	..	12 23	..	2 48	4 28	..	5 23	6 19	7 43	7 47	8 56	9 17	1222	..	5 12	8 38	..
57	Alresford	..	8 18	9 17	9 37	..	12 27	..	2 55	4 34	..	5P39	6 25	7Z54	7 54	9 1	9 24	1227	..	5 17	8 44	..
60¾	Itchen Abbas	..	8 24	9 23	9 43	..	12 33	..	3 3	4 40	..	5 45	6 31	8 0	8 0	9 7	9 30	1233	..	5 23	8 51	..
66½	Winchester City H arr.	..	8 35	9 34	9 55		12 46	..	3 15	4 51	..	5 56	6 42	8 11	8 11	9 18	9 41	1244	..	5 34	9 2	..
69¾	74 Shawford D arr	..	8 42	9 41	10 2	..	12 52	..	3 22	4 57	..	6 2	..	8 17	8 17	9 26	9 47	1250	..	..	9 9	..
73¼	74 Eastleigh F "	..	8 50	9 49	1010	..	1 0	..	3 30	5 4	..	6 9	..	8 25	8 25	9 34	9 55	1258	..	..	9 17	..
75¼	74 Swaythling "	..	..	..	..	..	..	..	..	5 13	..	..	..	..	..	..	10 5	..	..	..	9 24	..
77¼	74 St. Denys "	..	..	..	..	..	..	..	..	5 17	..	..	..	..	..	..	10 9	..	..	..	9 28	..
78¼	74 Northam "	..	..	..	..	..	..	..	..	5 21	..	..	..	..	..	..	..	..	..	..	..	..
79	74 Southampton G "	..	..	..	..	..	..	..	..	5 24	..	..	..	..	..	..	1015	..	..	..	9 34	..

Miles	Up	Week Days																Sundays					
		a.m	a.m	a.m	a.m	a.m	a.m	p.m	p.m	p.m	p.m	p.m	p.m	p.m	p.m	p.m	p.m	a.m	a.m		p.m	p.m	
	74 Southampton G dep	..	..	..	..	..	..	..	..	..	..	..	..	5 23	..	6 52	6 58	..	..	..	..	..	..
¾	74 Northam "	..	..	..	..	..	..	..	..	..	..	..	..	5 26	..	6 55	7 1	..	..	..	..	..	..
1¾	74 St. Denys "	..	..	..	..	..	..	..	..	..	..	..	..	5 30	..	6 59	7 5	..	..	..	..	..	..
3¼	74 Swaythling "	..	..	..	..	..	..	..	..	..	..	..	..	5 34	..	7 3	7 9	..	..	..	..	..	..
6½	74 Eastleigh F "	6 35	7 40	..	1016	1016	..	1 8	1 15	2 15	..	3 59	4 55	5 42	..	7 16	7 15	7 45	1046	..	3 42	..	..
9½	74 Shawford D "	6 42	7 47	..	1023	1023	..	1 15	1 22	2 22	..	4 6	5 2	5 52	..	7 24	7 22	7 52	1053	..	3 49	..	..
12¾	Winchester City H dep	6 50	7 56	..	1031	1031	..	1 22	1 29	2 29	..	4 14	5 9	6 5	..	7 32	7 32	7 59	11 0	..	3 56	7 27	..
18¼	Itchen Abbas	7 2	8 8	..	1044	1043	..	1 34	1 41	2 41	..	4 26	5 21	6 18	..	7 45	7 45	8 11	1112	..	4 8	7 33	..
22	Alresford	7 9	8 16	..	1051	1050	..	1 41	1 48	2d52	..	4 35	5 28	6 25	..	7 53	7 53	8 20	1119	..	4 15	7 43	..
24½	Ropley	7 16	8 23	..	1058	1057	..	1 48	1 55	3 0	..	4 42	5 35	6 32	..	8 0	8 0	8 27	1126	..	4 22	7 52	..
27½	Medstead & Four Marks	7 25	8 32	..	11 7	11 6	..	1 57	2 4	3 9	..	4 51	5 44	6 40	..	8 9	8 9	8 36	1135	..	4 31	8 1	..
32	Alton A arr.	7 34	8 41	..	1116	1115	..	2 6	2 13	3 18	..	5 0	5 52	6 49	..	8 18	8 18	8 45	1144	..	4 41	8 10	..
—	Mls Gosport dep.	..	..	7 42			1130			..	..	..	..	..	..			..	..	..	..	..	..
—	1½ Fort Brockhurst	..	..	7 45			1133			..	..	..	..	..	..			..	..	..	..	..	..
—	Mls Fareham dep.	..	..	7 57	Saturdays excepted	Saturdays only	1156	Saturdays only	Saturdays excepted	..	2 48	..	..	..	6 48	Saturdays only	Saturdays excepted	..	..	..	..	..	..
—	2 Knowle Halt	..	..	8 2			12 0			..	2 53	..	..	..	6 53			..	..	..	..	..	..
—	4½ Wickham	..	..	8 7			12 5			..	2 58	..	..	..	6 58			..	..	..	..	..	..
—	9¼ Droxford B	..	..	8 17			1215			..	3 8	..	..	..	7 8			..	..	..	..	..	..
—	13½ West Meon	..	..	8 25			1223			..	3 18	..	..	..	7 17			..	..	..	..	..	..
—	17¼ Privett	..	..	8 34			1232			..	3 29	..	..	..	7 27			..	..	..	..	..	..
—	20¼ Tisted	..	..	8 40			1238			..	3 36	..	..	..	7 34			..	..	..	..	..	..
—	22¼ Farringdon	..	..	8 44			1242			..	3 40	..	..	..	7 38			..	..	..	..	..	..
—	25¼ Alton A arr.	..	..	8 51			1249			..	3 47	..	..	..	7 46			..	..	..	..	..	..
79	Waterloo 76 arr	8 57	9B57	1016	1246	1254	2 17	3 45	3 46	4R46	5 16	6 46	7 16	8 16	9 16	9 46	9 46	1016	1 16	..	6 16	9 46	..

A Station for Selborne (4½ miles) B Station for Hambledon (3½ miles). B Arr. 10 16 a.m. on Saturdays.
D Station for Twyford. d Arr. 4 mins. earlier. F Station for Bishopstoke. G Southampton Terminus (for Docks)
H 1 mile from Winchester Chesil Station. K Dep. 4 27 p.m. on Saturdays. P Arr. 5 27 p.m.
R Arr. 4 45 p.m. on Saturdays. y 3 mins. later on Saturdays. Z Arr. 7 48 p.m. z 5 mins. later on Saturdays.

LOCAL TRAINS between Knowle Halt and Fareham, Table 73—Fareham and Gosport, Table 73.
OTHER TRAINS between London and Southampton, see Table 45

1953 public timetable

One particular working spoken of and which was supposedly photographed - although a copy cannot be located - was when a Bulleid pacific was seen north of West Meon viaduct on a short notice diversion from Portsmouth. The circumstances are not clear, although it is believed the reason was an obstruction on the intended route via Petersfield. Whatever, the type of engine was clearly prohibited by weight from travelling over the line. It is said an illustration of the event appeared in the staff magazine of the Pirelli cable company - this magazine had regular features of local interest on a variety of topics. Regretfully, and not withstanding a search through the available archives, nothing has been found. Possibly it occurred just before closure and at which point whoever was in charge of the diversion deemed that as the line was closing anyway such an event was of little consequence.

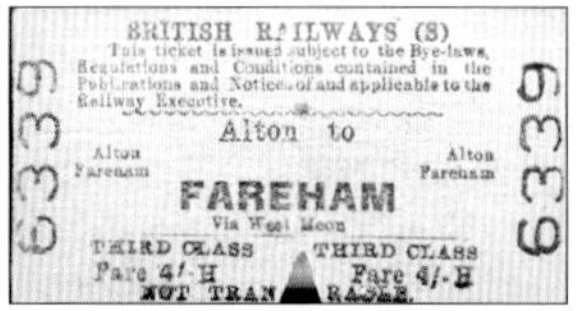

53. - *'T9' No 30726 at West Meon on 17 November 1954 with the down daily goods. This was the 9.20 am departure from Alton due to arrive at West Meon at 11.12. Here it was scheduled to spend 30 minutes attending to the traffic in the yard before leaving for Droxford at 12.42, where it would arrive eight minutes later. (At Droxford a crossing would be made with the 11.30 am ex-Gosport passenger push-pull service at 12.22 pm., the only train it would meet on its journey of more than six hours between Alton and Fareham.) On this occasion the load would appear to primarily that of beet - or is it potatoes? The down starting signal has been cleared for the train, although we cannot be certain if this is to allow it to pull forward before setting back into the yard, or at the conclusion of the work and it is ready to depart for Droxford. In reality it was probably the former, as witness the discussion taking place with the crew and the man standing on the remains of the weed covered down platform: probably giving instructions as to the shunt.*

Bluebell Railway Archive / J J Smith 5-111-5

54. - *Easter Monday, 19 April 1954. Shortly after 8.00 am, '700' class 0-6-0 No. 30308 waits at Droxford with the 7.38 Alton to Fareham passenger working. The train was due to arrive here at 8.12½ (the railway was always very pedantic about its half-minutes). This first train of the day was conventional locomotive hauled, and notwithstanding it was a bank-holiday, a normal weekday service of two morning and two afternoon trains would run, albeit the timings hardly conducive to encouraging custom. (By keeping the trains within approximately an eight-hour window, the line could be operated by the station staff and signalmen on a single shift.) At Droxford a crossing would be made with the 7.42 am from Gosport, similarly the first Up train of the day. No 30308 was due to depart at 8.18 and after calling at both Wickham and Knowle Halt would complete its journey at Fareham at 8.37 am. As an indication that the MV railway had already sunk into relative obscurity, there is no reference to any extra trains, excursions, or even additional coaches attached to the normal workings on that day.*

Bluebell Railway Archive / Colin Hogg 018-590

WALKING IN THE FOOTSTEPS OF HISTORY

55. - *Droxford early June 1944. Front row, left to right: Mr Mackenzie King (Prime Minister - Canada), (Sir) Winston Churchill, Mr Peter Fraser (Prime Minister - New Zealand), General Eisenhower, Sir Godfrey Huggins (Prime Minister - Southern Rhodesia), General Smuts (Prime Minister - South Africa and confident of Churchill). Post-war, a framed copy of this photograph hung in the booking office at Droxford but disappeared after closure in 1955 (the frame had been made at Eastleigh). The original was later presented to Mr Charles Anderson MBE.*

When the telephone rang in the office at Southampton Central station in June 1944 it was answered by Chares Anderson - Assistant District Traffic Inspector. The caller was from the wartime headquarters of the Southern Railway at Deepdene, near Dorking. "Expect a special train….must be to a place where it can stand unobtrusively for several days……...and have the protection of a cutting…." According to a 1963 report in the SOUTHERN EVENING ECHO this was how Churchill's train came to arrive at Droxford. No doubt there was slightly more to it than was reported, but what the same article does contain is a wonderful first hand report of the arrival and subsequent stabling of the special service, Droxford no doubt chosen not only because of its geographical advantages but also because of the close proximity to Southwick House and the fact that the Meon Valley line was not a major supply route, thus meaning wartime workings would not be affected. (Although it may be suspected the limited public passenger service was.*) Physically Wickham station was closer to Southwick by road but was rejected due to its relatively exposed location. Droxford had the advantage of a cutting to provide some physical protection as well a degree of visual obscurity by trees to one side. The Americans had offered to build a branch-line from Droxford into the hills at Southwick, but this was rejected.)

Continuing from the newspaper article, Anderson recalled the train arrived on Friday 2 June 1944, the photograph opposite shows it at the down platform implying it had arrived in the down direction. In all probability this was also the most likely - from London, but to be fair even if Mr Churchill and his entourage had come up from the south (inspecting troops perhaps) we may assume it would have been worked into the down platform anyway. (The last possibility is that the view was taken shortly before departure.) Whatever, that afternoon an eight-coach train of LMS vehicles in crimson livery, hauled by an SR 'T9' arrived - different reports refer to six vehicles. Rumours that had been circulating in the village beforehand - swarming with troops, police, and plain clothes security men - were now confirmed. The station especially was heavily guarded with the troops changed every four hours. With the train stopped Mr Churchill, in his customary siren suit, alighted on to the platform to be followed by a dignified man in Army tropical kit: General Smuts. Codenamed 'Rugged' this train was the mobile headquarters of the Prime Minister. Later the stock was shunted back into the up siding at Droxford where it was indeed protected by the cutting.

Charles Anderson's responsibility had not ended in the taking of the telephone call and suggested stabling point, he was also tasked with remaining with the train whilst it was at Droxford and to take responsibility for its safety and movement. Comfort was not spared, the formation included a 12-wheel sleeping car, a saloon, a day coach and office. Other vehicles provided accommodation for visiting 'guests'. As more 'guests' than normal were expected, an additional sleeping car was secured from the LNER (the Southern did not possess such vehicles), it was in this vehicle that Anderson and other Southern Railway staff were billeted, enjoying the same VIP food as was served to the principal occupants of the train. Immediately the train was placed in its siding, GPO engineers were on-hand to connect the Prime Minister's private telephone to London.

The following day, 3 June, Anthony Eden and Ernest Bevin arrived by car. More VIPS were expected later, namely the Soviet and US ambassadors. Their arrival was at first watched for by an aide, Cmdr. Thompson, but he was recalled to the train and the job was given to Insp. Thompson, Churchill's 'shadow'. He however got fed up with waiting and passed it on to Charles Anderson, in the event neither turned up.

June 4 saw even more arrivals, according to the newspaper reports, all by car. At first these were various military men and government officials but shortly afterwards the remainder of the senior players arrived, the Canadian Premier: Mackenzie King, the Prime Minister of New Zealand: Peter Fraser, and Sir Godfrey Huggins of Southern Rhodesia. The last two to arrive at Droxford were General Eisenhower and General de Gaulle. At this point the men went into conference in the train - no one, save the engine driver and fireman, now allowed closer than 50 yards.* At the conclusion many of the VIPS, excepting at least Churchill departed by car. The villagers of Droxford would later claim it was at this conference that the decision was made to stage D-Day on 6 June, one day later than had been originally been planned. (When the occupants of the train wished to leave the stabled train - see image of actual location at No. 111 - instructions were shouted to the engine crew who would draw forward into the up platform, the VIPS having to cross the line and exit via the booking hall into their respective waiting cars. Mr Churchill did not bother with such refinements, he would walk through the goods yard.)

Anderson now received orders for the train to return to London, although there was no decision as to whether this should be to Waterloo or Kensington. In the event Cmdr. Thompson and Anderson tossed a coin - Waterloo won. Departure was at 6.58 pm, immediately behind the 6.56 pm ex Portsmouth service. The latter being shunted at Tisted to allow the special to pass.

*The train engine would have been serviced at either Eastleigh or Fratton although before this happened a spare engine was in readiness in the yard at all times. Water was of course available at West Meon. There is also a report of a mess van being provided in the yard. Once 'in-conference' no one was allowed within 50 yards, so does this mean other traffic was stopped - or indeed had been throughout the stay of the train? (The special train was stabled within a few feet of the normal running line - see illustrations Nos. 57 & 111.) Clearly when travelling, 'Rugged' would be given a priority rating with other trains held, but in a stationary scenario we cannot be certain if other traffic was allowed to pass.) It would have been a simple matter to instigate a substitute bus service from West Meon to Wickham so by-passing Droxford, similar arrangements having been applied on other lines whenever engineering work or other necessity demanded. Possibly normal working was allowed except when 'in conference'. Finally, with the Prime Minister on board, surely it would have been sensible to allow the special to depart ahead of the service train, that is assuming he was ready! So far as 'ordinary' wartime traffic on the line was concerned, according to Ray Stone, a box van was added to every passenger train to cater for extra parcels and troops' luggage. Unless conventional loco working was applied, this would have increased considerably the time at the end of each journey performing the necessary shunt moves.

"On Manoeuvres by the Meon Valley line"

MECHANISED CAVALRY

56. - This intriguing photograph came to light by pure chance in a box of old War Office photos at a military bookseller's stand at the Bovington Tank Museum.

The location is the Hedge Corner road junction on the A32 Alton to Fareham road between East Tisted and Privett, this despite the fact that the bridge has long been demolished. Similarly the adjacent embankments have also been levelled although a clue as to the location can still be gained in the 21st century by the presence of a lay-by either side of the present day junction and which was once the course of the original A32 prior to being straightened. As depicted here, the main A32 runs left to right under the bridge, with the Alton direction to the right. The junction was in effect a staggered crossroads at this point and in the immediate foreground part of the Petersfield road. Opposite the road leading towards Monkwood and Ropley can be seen.

Just out of sight on the right hand side of the bridge at the top of the embankment, was an open fronted timber lean-to shelter, used by the permanent-way department to store a motorised trolley.

The photo bears the caption 'Mechanised Cavalry' and is a wonderful study of different elements of a mechanised cavalry unit on exercise shortly before WW2. Light tanks, tank crew, a signals truck and a despatch rider are all pictured. So who were they? The clue to the unit's identity is the regimental badge on the side of the turret of the tank in the left of the photograph. Under a magnifying glass, the shape of the badge appears to match that of the 4th Queens Own Hussars

The regimental history of the 4th Queen's Own Hussars states that the regiment was mechanised in 1936, initially trading its horses for lorries. In November 1937, less than two years before the outbreak of WW2, the regiment took delivery of its first tanks, the Vickers Mark VIB light tank, as seen in the photo. At this time, the regiment was based at Aldershot, transferring to Tidworth in October 1938 with 1st Cavalry Brigade. Given the leaves on the trees in the photo and the greater likelihood of the unit being 'on manoeuvres' from Aldershot rather than Tidworth, the photo was almost certainly taken in 1938.

A similar photograph is located on the Imperial War Museum website, although there it is described as involving the Royal Tank Corps. This cannot be correct, as the uniforms of the two were significantly different at the time. Indeed, at first glance, to non-military enthusiasts, the tank crewmen's uniforms bear a certain similarity to those of the German Panzertruppen. The thought that this might have been joint manoeuvres can be instantly discounted; had we of course been invaded, then scenes like this might have been all too familiar. (Although details are sparse, mention may be made of two special trains known to have used the line in WW2. The first was in 1941 from Swallowcliffe to Droxford and was run to assess the practicality of movement of both men and weaponry in the same train. Motive power was provided by a '700' class 0-6-0 hauling six coaches plus 35 bren-gun carriers loaded on to flat wagons. The train remained at Droxford for two days, stabled in the long siding - the same one as would later be used by Churchill - vacuum brake trouble delaying its scheduled departure for the coast by several hours. The second train referred to arrived at Tisted from the north and was shunted into the long siding there overnight, the engine crew instructed to be ready for move off at daylight. Two days later the staff on line learnt that what had been stored and then travelled under their noses - sea mines.)

WALKING IN THE FOOTSTEPS OF HISTORY

57. - In August 1950 six years after Churchill's visit, 'Picture Post' sent their photographer Bert Hardy to revisit the scene. In what is clearly a posed view, Porter / Signalmen Bert McRill (left) and Reg Gould, who were on duty on the occasion in June 1944, are seen walking on to the up siding where the train was held. The single line over which service trains would pass is on the right. (As might be expected with a press visit, it was normal for more than one image to be recorded and having located this view there were high hopes for others of the station of a similar quality taken at the same time. Unusually it was unique.) A note on the back of the file print within the archive also records two simple words, 'Story Killed'. Perhaps just six years after the event it was still meant to be Droxford's secret. Getty Archive 98087991

War came to Droxford twice in the 1940s. The first time was on 18 April 1941 when after a bad night for the railway in the Portsmouth area (346 tons of high explosive and over 46,000 incendiary devices were dropped) at 11.50 am, "...considerable damage was done to the station and line at Droxford". No further detail is given. Then at 4.30 pm on 5 November 1942 the 1.05 pm Fareham to Alton freight (evidently running somewhat late) was machine-gunned while in Droxford station although (officially) no damage was done to the train or station. In reality a Junkers 88 did cause some light damage to the station building as well demolishing two of the station cottages. The aircraft continued down the valley and dropped further bombs south of the station near Soberton: these fell either side of the track. Even so communication with Wickham was cut and pilot-man working was in place for 24 hours. (On the same day and either just before or afterwards, the same aircraft flew over West Meon station - causing two coalmen weighing coal to dive for cover - before dropping another bomb intended for the north portal of West Meon tunnel. Fortunately it missed but some track and sleepers were damaged as well as Vinnels Lane Bridge. Fortunately telephone communication was intact and an urgent call to Privett managed to stop the 4.30 pm passenger service from Alton. Years later Ganger Harold Shawyer recalled the second incident, "Shunting a freight train we were. He came over the trees and dropped a stick of bombs up the line. Didn't do any damage though except a few bullet holes in the station brickwork. He might have done better had he come over in June 1944." This was the only known incident to affect the Meon Valley line in WW2 although elsewhere locally, Alton and especially Fareham were affected. There was also an incident on 19 August 1942 when a passenger train was machine-gunned approaching Alresford and whilst at the latter station. Minor damage was done to the locomotive but fortunately there were no casualties. (On the night of 10/11 March 1941 a heavy raid took place which, amongst other damage, resulted in Gosport station being gutted by fire. Amongst the damage was a wagon load of furniture belonging to the station master, loaded and ready to depart. He had been due to move to Wickham the very next day.)

A RURAL BACKWATER

58 - How the mighty have fallen. Once perhaps intended as a through route between London and Gosport, even an alternative main line to Portsmouth, this scene at West Meon on Saturday 13 November 1954, typifies the railway in what was its last full year of operation - six months later trains would no longer call at West Meon. The locomotive, 'T9' No 30726, had been built in 1899 for the London & South Western Railway, one of a class intended for express and other prestige workings. Gradually newer and more modern machines would take its place so that by the 1930s it and its type were downgraded, in the main, to lesser workings. Twenty years on from then and it is seeing out its time shunting West Meon goods yard. The station too: neat yes, but with little sign of much pending business. The platform edges have been neatly whitened - a WW2 feature that would be continued in later years, although there was no point in so identifying the now unused section of platform at the south end. Look carefully on the Up platform and the running-in board proclaiming the station name 'West Meon', was never moved from the unused portion. Years earlier in September 1933, the 'SOUTHERN RAILWAY MAGAZINE' had devoted a full page to a farm removal from West Meon. "These pictures (the railway images were all taken at West Meon) show various stages in the biggest farm removal ever performed in the south of England, which was carried out by the Southern Railway, when the whole of the household furniture, farm machinery, implements, live stock, etc., of a farm at Brockwood Park, West Meon, together with about 14 passengers,

was conveyed by two special trains to Frith House, Stalbridge, Dorset. The train loads comprised 19 containers loaded with household furniture, 13 wagons of machinery and implements, 50 sheep and lambs, 17 cows, 13 heifers and calves, 9 horses, 2 bulls and 1 goat. The running of one of the trains was so arranged so as to allow of the cows being milked at their usual time overnight on the farm at West Meon and also in the morning at Stalbridge." (Images 59-64.)

Bluebell Railway Museum, J J Smith 5-111-2

Top - 65. - *Busy times at Alton and not an electric train in sight! 'M7' No. 30032 waits in Platform 2 with a Mid Hants line service formed of conventional stock - in appearance a 3-coach set of LSWR origin. On the right is the rear end of a Meon Valley push-pull working recently arrived and with the tail-lamp still in place. (The single headcode disc ready for the return working is also in place.) The MV stock is set No 36, at this time, c1950, in regular use on the MV line. By 1954 the same set had moved and was based at Bournemouth West. In the same year, 1954, set No. 31 is shown as being solely used on the line, commencing its booked working from Eastleigh at 5.39 am whence it ran to Fareham. Eastleigh also had push-pull sets Nos 1-6 and No. 662. Any one of these might be used on MV services although it was practice to keep two sets for relief with No. 662 spare.*

Bottom left - 66. - *The northern end of the Meon Valley line looking towards Butts Junction from Bridge No. 1. (The latter was known as 'Mounter's Lane Bridge' and carried the railway over a public road.) On the left hand side may be seen the embankment carrying the Mid Hants line, the steam coming from a Mid Hants train that may just be discerned in the distance. Interesting is the use of steel sleepers on this section of the MV route. These were in place here as well as for some distance between Butts Junction and Alton (not of course a physical junction since 1935 although the name persisted). Ray Stone comments that according to legend, and at the time when there was physical junction for the three lines and of course a working signal box, on occasions the signalman was so busy he would cook his breakfast but not have time to eat it. The present author would agree with Ray's obvious doubts. Such a statement was indeed true at a busy main line box, but with the sporadic service on at least two of the three routes plus the fact that only one train might be present on each single line at a time, the conclusion must be the signalman may have been a very slow eater!*

Denis Cullum 2397

Below - 67. & 68. - *Two separate types of steel sleeper were used in places on the line: from illustrations, it would appear mainly at the northern end.*

69. - *Farringdon goods siding and halt, the latter opened as 'Farringdon' from 1 May 1931. It was renamed 'Faringdon Platform' exactly a year later on 1 May 1932 and changed again to 'Farringdon' from 8 July 1934. Of clearly limited length, passengers intending to alight here were requested to travel in the front coach. The lack of any shelter for intending passengers will be noted. On the right is a trolley hut for the ganger's motorised trolley - see notes photo No. 121. The view is looking south, towards Tisted, on 3 February 1955.* Denis Cullum 2399

Top - 70. - *Evening sunshine at Farringdon with a British Railways lorry awaiting its next days work. Farringdon was a railhead for the villages in the area, the lorry no doubt also visiting the neighbouring stations as required. The original goods facilities are shown here and consisted of just the two sidings: the 'main-line' is visible on the extreme left between the wagons. From 19 December 1932 an additional siding for Messrs. Aylward was added north of the under bridge the parapet of which may just be seen in image No. 69. Sometime in WW2 a second siding was provided off this - both on the east side of the line. To control access, a second ground frame was provided, 13 chains north of the original - see image No. 72. It is not known how long either of these newer sidings remained in use.*

David Ballard

Left - 71. - *The goods shed at Farringdon and of identical style to those originally provided at all of the MV line stations. Some advertising is provided both on the outside walls and within and so indicating passengers may well have sheltered here at times. Notwithstanding its lowly status, tickets were also issued from here.*

Denis Cullum 2401

Left (main view) - 72. - Looking back towards the original two sidings - the additional facilities are just beyond the bridge (inset). Control of these new, gated, sidings was from an open-air 2-lever ground frame. The original ground frame hut was of an LSWR standard type and identical to that at Mislingford: it contained four levers. The name 'Farringdon' was displayed on a large wooden board above the front windows parallel to the running line. Release was by inserting the tablet for the Alton (Butts Junction) to Tisted section after which the respective levers to operate the siding could be reversed. The points had to be restored to the single line and the facing point lock placed 'in' before the tablet could be removed. There was no facility for crossing trains. Denis Cullum 1510

(Inset - 72A. - A cruel enlargement from a similar image but showing the divergence of the second siding.)

Bottom - 73. - A light load for '700' class No 30308 bound for Farringdon with goods from Alton. By the early 1950s, this was one of only three types of engine regularly seen on the line, the others being examples of the T9' and 'M7' classes. V B Orchard

TISTED

Top left - 74. - *Tisted, looking west towards the railway from the Tisted to Selborne road. On the immediate left, the road led to the goods yard, the roadway leading to the station entrance is under the bridge on the left. The railway staff cottages are out of sight on the immediate right.* The South Western Circle

Top right - 75. *- The exterior of Tisted station. Down the line the stations, and consequently the signalboxes, were placed on alternate sides, although in the case of the former this was a matter of necessity. On the extreme right the roadway continues over the bridge seen in No. 79 in the direction of Colemore.*

Norman Simmons

Left - 76. *- From the north looking through the station towards Privett. The nameboard displays the dual name, although certainly in later years, Alton would equally offer its facilities as being convenient for Selbourne. As with the other stations, the concrete platforms were 600' long although it is doubtful if these were ever alongside a 10-coach train. The signal box contained a frame of 23 levers. The up and down distant signals at Tisted were changed from red to yellow arms on 27 April 1928 and it may well have been at this time that were altered to be 'fixed'. In later years the lever frame included 8 spare levers.*

Top left - 77. - *From the vantage point of the embankment on the east side of the road overbridge, looking down upon the station and yard. The box van is stands alongside the cattle pens on what also used to be the goods shed siding, the latter formerly where the trees are sprouting. This is a post November 1950 view, by which time some rationalisation had been made to the yard and its track access.*

Top right - 78. - *Post 1950 looking north towards Farringdon. On the left and centre are the platform lines - combining into one in the near distance. On the right is the access into the yard as well as the long headhunt (officially the down siding) where, due to the gradient, goods trains were supposed to stand during shunting. The down home signal is of the upper-quadrant type.* Norman Simmons

Right - 79. - *A final view between the platforms at Tisted with its clearly smoke-blackened bridge. Despite the derelict appearance the line was still open. Under the canopy it is possible to glimpse the up starting signal (No. 3 in the frame) and at this time of LSWR lower-quadrant type. It would be changed before closure, probably on the basis of scheduled renewal: see image No. 80.*

Top left - 80. - *From the yard side, the crane and rear of the signal box. A permanent way gang was based at Tisted - hence the concrete huts seen in the yard in No. 77. The gang here were responsible for 11 miles of line from Butts Junction as far as West Meon Viaduct, including the two tunnels. The ten-man Tisted gang were the recipients of an award for the best kept permanent-way on at least two occasions, in 1949 and 1950. Wilfred Pink was the ganger at the time. (see No. 91.) In the far corner the replacement upper-quadrant starting signal can be seen.*

The South Western Circle

Top right, 81. - *Water for the station was drawn from a well and stored in the tank - a cast plate affixed to the side proclaimed 'LSWR Wimbledon Works'. As well as the station house, this would have supplied the gents toilet and also a water supply to the cattle pens - possibly even the staff cottages. The South Western Circle*

Left - 82. - *The entrance to a weed strewn yard with the abutment of the overbridge seen in No. 74 on the left. As well as a crane, a loading gauge was provided at each of the station yards.*

The South Western Circle

Below - *Maintenance example from 1914.*

MEON VALLEY (ALTON AND FAREHAM) LINE.

No. 81.—The Engineer will have possession of the undermentioned Electric Train Tablet Circuits, on the dates and between the times shewn, for the purpose of cleaning and overhauling the Electric Train Tablet instruments :—

Electric Train Tablet Section.	Date and Hours.	Remarks.
Butts Junction (Alton) and Tisted.	From 9.50 a.m. on Tuesday, 9th June, until completed the same day.	Mr. Ewings, Tisted, to arrange pilot working.

Pilot working to be carried out in accordance with Regulation No. 27, of the Standard Block Regulations for Single Lines worked on the Electric Train Tablet system.

Left - 83. - *From the overbridge viewed south over a pair of grass strew platforms - the railway still in operation at this time. The two signal are again of replacement upper-quadrant type. At all the stations on the Meon Valley line only one train could be admitted to the station at one time, a crossing movement whereby trains arrived at the same time would see one held until the first had arrived. In practice the signalman would usually wait and clear the line for whichever was the first to announce its presence by whistling.*

Bottom - 84. - *Northbound between Privett and Tisted, not far from Hedge Corner (see No. 56) with the A32 alongside. The train is the 2.48 pm from Fareham to Alton, which would put the time just after 3.30 pm - see timetable opposite Nos 53 / 54. 'M7' No. 30054 has charge of a 2-coach 'push-pull' set, on this occasion being 'pulled'. Two more regular passenger trains would traverse the line that day, one in the down direction and a final up service four hours after the train seen. Locomotives for most Meon Valley services, certainly in later years, came from either Guildford or Fratton. Some Eastleigh men however also had route knowledge of the line. 19 June 1954.* Denis Cullum 2122

PRIVETT

85. - *Privett, looking as much like a country house as a station. This view clearly shows the separate entrances to the passenger station and goods yard. The building is a mirror image of that at Tisted, the purpose of which was to have the entrance hall nearest arriving passengers. The right hand end of the main building contained the station offices, with the 'Gentlemen's facilities as an almost separate structure. The exterior door beyond the canopy provided access to the private quarters. With its deep-set windows and wide stone surrounds to these, the whole presents what might even be described as a heavy, even gothic appearance. 19 June 1954.*

Denis Cullum 2124

86. - *Seemingly busy times at Privett probably after the departure of the last down train from Alton - at 4.48 pm. The number present indicates this may have been market day at Alton which always resulted in extra passengers. Reduced price tickets were available to Alton for this purpose. With no signalman present, a bell under the canopy was rung to announce the pending arrival of trains, this was operated by the signalman at either Tisted or West Meon, dependent upon the direction of travel. In the booking office, and possibly in the ground frame, there was telephone communication with the stations on either side.*

87 - *No. 30693. a '700' class 0-6-0 arrives at the station with the daily up goods, Tuesday 28 December 1954. Privett was the high point on the railway, the line dropping on both sides at 1-660 and then at 1-100: in the southbound direction this gradient continued some four miles all the way to West Meon. The canopy supports display their wartime alternate black / white paint, it was never removed before closure. Either side of the station yellow marker lights replaced the distant signals consequent upon the abolition of the signal box in 1922. These were illuminated by paraffin oil which were replenished at intervals by the porter-in-charge. Almost opposite the engine, there was a gap in the fencing allowing pedestrian access into the goods yard.*

Bluebell Railway Museum, J J Smith 5-115-3

Below - *Maintenance example from 1914.*

MEON VALLEY (ALTON AND FAREHAM LINE.

No. 120. Retimbering points and crossings at Tisted Station.

This work will be in progress in the down and up loop lines from 12.5 a.m. on **Sunday, 14th June** until **further notice** at intervals between trains, during which time the various points and signals will be disconnected as required.

Mr. Ewings to provide flagmen as required.

No. 121.—The Engineer will have possession of the undermentioned Electric Train Tablet Circuits, on the dates and between the times shewn, for the purpose of cleaning and overhauling the Electric Train Tablet instruments :—

Electric Train Tablet Section.	Date and Hours.	Remarks.
Butts Junction (Alton) and Tisted.	From 9.15 a.m. on **Wednesday, 17th June**, until completed the same day.	Mr. Ewings, Tisted, to arrange pilot working.
Tisted and Privett.	From 9.30 a.m. on **Thursday, 18th June**, until completed the same day.	Mr. Ewings, Tisted, to arrange pilot working.
Privett and West Meon.	From 9.30 a.m. on **Friday, 19th June**, until completed the same day.	Mr. Delia, Privett, to arrange pilot working.

Pilot working to be carried out in accordance with Regulation No. 27, of the Standard Block Regulations for Single Lines worked on the Electric Train Tablet system.

Left - 88. - *Viewed from the south with the lead in to what was a 37 chain curve at the start of the platform - the sharpest curve on any part of the running line on the MV route. This did ease slightly to 47 chain radius at the north end of the platform. From this angle the basic track layout is apparent, the former up platform now used as a goods run-round loop with the up siding nearest the camera on the immediate left. On the right is the headshunt from the goods yard. The track layout had been simplified slightly in consequence of the 1922 downgrading. In both this and the lower view, the staff cottages, alongside the present day A32, are visible: top right. Notice also the standard SR concrete p/way huts, from their clean appearance it would appear these were new at several locations on the line in the early 1950s. 19 June 1954 Denis Cullum 2125*

Bottom left - 89. - *The former signal box, seen here in use as a ground-frame. As with Tisted, this had originally contained a Stevens' 23 lever frame with six spare levers. The 1922 alterations saw the facing points locks altered to stand 'in' as their normal position. Although not confirmed it is likely nine levers remained operated from the ground-frame, one turnout in the yard controlled by an adjacent hand lever. A train may be seen, probably arriving, at what is a deserted platform. 18 December 1954.*

S C Nash

No. 91.--Relaying works, &c., in progress until further notice.

LINE.	AT OR BETWEEN.	DESCRIPTION OF WORK.	INSTRUCTIONS AND SPEED RESTRICTIONS.
Meon Valley (Alton and Fareham).	Butts Junction (Alton) and Tisted.	Repairing brickwork of bridges Nos. 1, 4, 5, 6, 7, 8, 9, 10, 11, 12, 13 and 14.	Drivers to look out for hand signals.
	Butts Junction (Alton) and Tisted, 52 and 54 mile posts.		
	Tisted and Privett, 54 and 57 mile posts.	Adjusting rails in single line.	Completed.
	Privet and West Meon, 57¾ and 61¾ mile posts.		

Left - 90. - *Bridge No. 25, at Privett, also the location from where No. 88 was taken. There is more than sufficient room for the single running line, right, and the up siding - the latter around 600' in length. The difference in levels is apparent, the running line falling at 1 in 100 after a more gentle 1 in 600 in the immediate station area. Had the railway ever been doubled, there would still have been a need for the up siding, hence the bridge was built to span three tracks although for this the cutting would have required some excavation. Privett station is just beyond the curve.*

Bottom - 91. - *Presentation at Privett. Mr V A M Robertson, Chief Civil Engineer Southern Region presenting an award to the Tisted permanent way gang at Privett in 1950. (Why this should be done at Privett and not Tisted is not clear - possibly the men were working at Privett on that day.) Ganger Wilfred Pink is seen being congratulated for the best kept length of track in the central division of the SR. In addition to a certificate, this was worth £34 to the gang. Besides Wilfred Pink, those present include, William Pink, Leonard and Sydney Jackson, William Coutts, Harold Appleton, Charles Hunt, Edward Bounre, Ernest Bundy and James Bullen. On the extreme left it is believed is Inspector Turner from Alton.*   *Bob Winkworth collection*

Top left - 92. - Between Privett and West Meon. Push-pull set No. 3, with both driver and guard riding in the front vestibule and pushed by 'M7, No. 30047, has just left Privett tunnel heading south for West Meon with the 1.30 pm from Alton . Southbound passenger trains were allowed seven minutes for the four mile journey between the two stations. In the up direction and with the gradient against the engine all the way, the allowance was nine minutes. Passenger trains would also stop at all stations. The hoop with the single line tablet can be identified in the right hand carriage window. 13 November 1954.
Bluebell Railway Museum, J J Smith 5-111-6

Bottom left - 93. - On the same day, the 12.23 freight from Fareham to Alton is seen working hard behind No. 30327 as it climbs north over the viaduct at West Meon. This is one of the longest freight trains we see in photographs on the line and may have consisted of wagons of sugar beet - the eventual destination for which was either Kidderminster or one of the East Anglian processing plants. Beet was collected in the yard at West Meon and when there was a suitable number of wagons ready to despatch the station master would contact the Southampton control office either to arrange a special working or have the wagons attached to what might have otherwise been a lightly loaded freight daily freight. The maximum loading for any freight train on the line was 40 wagons, dependent upon the engine type, and whilst the train seen was probably just over half of this amount, it would still present a stiff task climbing to the summit at Privett.   Bluebell Railway Museum, J J Smith 5-111-7

Above - 94. - The Eastleigh bridge gang seen here at the north end of West Meon viaduct. The occasion is not reported but certainly included some painting .   Bob Winkworth collection.

95. - *'T9' No 30726 between the viaduct and West Meon station with the 9.20 freight from Alton to Fareham, 13 November 1954. (See also No. 99.) Two years earlier the timing had this train running one hour later. In 1954 it would cross the corresponding daily up freight working at Wickham, both freights workings also shown as serving Mislingford siding, this meant the latter location had a second freight train arrive less than 30 minutes after the first one had departed. In the photograph, the course of the line can be followed with the chalk face of the south end of West Meon tunnel also identifiable. The train load here would appear to be one of potatoes. The sugar beet workings referred to at No. 93, could see movement off the valley either north or south, Southampton control routing these on any number of different lines. West Meon may also have been a collecting point for odd wagons loaded elsewhere on the line and held here until there was sufficient to warrant movement. (Some sugar beet trains destined for Kidderminster would be assembled at either Bevois Park or Eastleigh and then run via the DNS line on to the Western Region.)*
Bluebell Railway Museum, J J Smith 5-111-7

96. - *The 10.30 is seen again pulling out of the yard at West Meon on 4 December 1954, this time with a more substantial load. The engine is 'T9' No. 30705.*

S C Nash

97. - *A sad comparison with images No. 2 and 28. The forecourt at West Meon presents a decidedly dejected appearance on 1 January 1955. Access to the station was via a steep roadway leading off the appropriately named Station Road. This driveway then took a sharp right turn to approach the forecourt. Yard access was through the gates at the end of the building. The railway would survive just five more weeks. West Meon station was built in the same orientation as at Tisted.*

Denis Cullum 2348

98. - *'T9' No. 30708 with a short freight at West Meon in 1949. Rumour has it that certain engine crews would take advantage of the leisurely schedules applicable to both passenger and especially freight services, running fast between stations with the intention of arriving early at their next stop. The purpose was to enjoy a visit to a local hostelry, each of the Meon Valley stations being conveniently located. There appears to some activity under the canopy although apart from this there is little in the way of traffic.*

Edward Griffiths

99. - *Busy time at West Meon, Saturday 13 November 1954. 'M7' No. 30047 awaits departure with the 11.56 am Fareham to Alton - due to depart West Meon at 12.23½ pm. (Prior to the closure of the Gosport line to passengers in June 1953, this train had started from that point. Out of sight, but in the yard, is No. 30726 (see No. 95) which was in charge of the down goods on that day - four wagons from which are stabled in the down platform. Seen on what was a bright autumn day, the location displays a vibrant appearance. Notice also the up-home signal in the distance is in the 'off' position. As with Tisted, a few years earlier in 1949, both this and the corresponding down home signal had been of the lower quadrant type but were replaced sometime between 1949 and 1954. (See No. 98.)*

Bluebell Railway Archive / J J Smith 5-111-3

Top - 100. - Wednesday 9 June 1954 and the last train up the valley for that day. '700' No. 30308 arrives with the a van and three coaches forming the 6.48 pm Fareham to Alton, due at West Meon at 7.16½ pm. There was nothing else to travel south on that day so after a pause of just one minute it would leave northbound. Meanwhile once 'out of section' had been given to Droxford, the signalman at that location could go home. The West Meon man would have to wait until the service reached Tisted around 7.33 pm before he too could finish for the day. The neat garden in front of the signal was a feature here for many years. The signal box contained 25 levers, with six spares, and was the longest frame on the line. Denis Cullum 2131

Bottom - 101. - The advantage of working for the railway, as Denis Cullum did, was the privileges it afforded: such as using the up home signal as a high vantage point from which to record this birds-eye view of West Meon from the south. On the right is the main running line, diverging into two to form the platform lines. In the centre is the up siding - the elongated sleeper spacing of which will be noted. Note also the extremely sharp curve from the headshunt - far left and on which the wagons are standing - leading into the yard. The seemingly complex access and exit from the goods yard was similarly applied at all the stations and was necessary due to an intolerance of having facing points in passenger lines whenever possible. 1 January 1955. Denis Cullum 2351

For reasons now lost in the midst of time, some minor signalling alterations are noted at West Meon from 1943 onwards.

"On Wednesday 21 July 1943, the down home signal was moved 7 yards farther from the signal box and raised to 17½ feet above rail level.

"On Thursday 22 July 1943 it was reported that the up home signal had already been moved to a new location 25 yards further south, no date for this alteration is given.

"On 6 May 1948 is was reported that the catch points in No. 1 siding, formerly situated 177 yards Droxford side of the signal box had been moved 12 yards farther from the signal box.

"On 9 May 1948, the shunting signal 62 yards Droxford side of the signal box, controlling movements from up line to No. 1 or 2 up siding, will be moved to a new position between down and up lines opposite its present site, and apply as hitherto.

"On Sunday 14 November 1948, the shunting signal, 128 yards the Droxford side of the signal box, controlling movements from No. 2 up siding to the up line, will be moved to a new position on the left hand side of No. 2 siding, 7 yards father from the signal box, and apply as hitherto."

Top - 102. - *The exterior of Droxford from Station Road. Here the wide forecourt only provided access to the passenger station, with access to the goods yard via a roadway on the east side of the line, this diverged from the Droxford to Hambledon road. Notwithstanding the poster boards still proclaiming 'Southern', the image dates from 1 January 1955. The top of the wind pump may just be seen above the roofline at the right of the main building.*

Denis Cullum 2356

Bottom - 103. *- Mid-day at Droxford. No 30305 has charge of the up goods whilst in the down platform an M7 is on a down service. The trains concerned are the 2.04 pm passenger departure from Droxford to Fareham and the 2.18 pm goods to Alton, The fact the engine of the freight train is at its head and the train appears complete, may indicate work had been completed and the freight will depart for West Meon ahead of time. With just four passenger workings each way over the Meon Valley line in its last years this might justifiably be considered a restricted service. Spare a thought however, for the then passenger service between Fareham and Gosport, with just two trains each way in the final timetable before closure.*

Opposite - *What may well be the original signal diagram from Droxford signal box, removed upon closure and fortunately found years later. As can be seen the frame contained 24 levers, and in 1948 - the date of the diagram - seven spares. Nos 1 and 24 would originally have been the down and up distant signals respectively. (Red distant signals were substituted by yellow here on Tuesday 1 May 1928 - at West Meon on Monday 30 April and at Wickham on Wednesday 2 May - possibly the time they were also 'fixed'.) Here, as well as at West Meon and Wickham, limited electrical locking was provided. One specific signalling alteration is referred to at Droxford, on 22 July 1943, when it was reported that the up home signal (No. 23), had been moved 21 yards farther from the signal box and lowered to 19 feet above rail level. As at the other stations, upper quadrant signal arms replaced the original lower quadrant type early in BR days. Note the unusual design of drawing used to indicate the Facing Point Locks (Nos. 7 & 14). Finally, it may be mentioned that Mr. Churchill's train was stabled on what is referred to as 'Up Siding No. 1' - although it should be noted this is not scaled on the drawing. The thick lines indicate passenger running lines.* Pat Butler

BRITISH RAILWAYS — SOUTHERN REGION

DROXFORD

WEST MEON

WICKHAM

DOWN LOOP →
← UP LOOP

SIGNAL BOX.

UP SIDING Nº 1

UP SIDING Nº 2

ELEVATED FRAME.
CLOSING SWITCH :- NIL.
Nº 6 TABLET.
POINTS MECHANICALLY DETECTED :- 9. 10. 11. 12.
WHITE LIGHT GROUND SIGNALS :- 17. 18. 19. 20.
RED LIGHT GROUND SIGNALS :- 21.
ALL DISTANCES IN YARDS FROM CENTRE OF BOX.

MECHANICAL LOCKING / ELECTRICAL LOCKING & DETECTION.

DISTANCES	Nº	DESCRIPTION	RELEASED BY	WORK.	LOCKING	WORK	NORMAL LOCK TABLET "OUT" TO.	RELEASED BY DETECTION MECHANICAL	POINT BOLTS "IN"	LOCKS
S	1.			1.					
232	2.	DOWN HOME.	7.	2.	10. 11. 19. 21. 23.	2.			(7)
73	3.	DOWN STARTING.	13.	3.	10.	3.	WICKHAM		
5	4.			4.		4.			
5	5.			5.		5.			
5	6.			6.		6.			
212	7.	F.P.L ON 8.		7.	8.	7.			
212	8.	DOWN LOOP POINTS.		8.	7.	8.			
73 · 137	9.	UP SIDING Nº 2 TO UP LINE POINTS.		9.	10. 11. 12.	9.			
81 · 154	10.	UP SIDING Nº 2 TO DOWN LINE POINTS.	13.	10.	2. 3. 9. 11. 12.	10.			
134	11.	UP TO DOWN LINE POINTS.		11.	2. 9. 10. 12. 13.	11.			
186	12.	UP SIDING Nº 1 CATCH POINTS.		12.	9. 10. 11.	12.			
203	13.	UP LOOP POINTS.		13.	11. 14.	13.			
203	14.	F.P.L ON 13.		14.	13.	14.			
5	15.			15.		15.			
5	16.			16.		16.			
72	17.	UP LINE TO UP SIDINGS GROUND SIGNAL.	(9 OR 12)	17.	19. 21. 22.	17.		(9) OR 9.11.	
80	18.	UP SIDING Nº 2 TO DOWN LINE GROUND SIGNAL.	10.	18.	20.	18.	WICKHAM	(10)	
138	19.	UP SIDING Nº 2 TO UP LINE GROUND SIGNAL.	9.	19.	2. 17.	19.		(9)	
155	20.	DOWN LINE TO UP SIDING Nº 2 GROUND SIGNAL.	10.	20.	18.	20.		(10)	
187	21.	UP SIDING Nº 1 TO UP LINE GROUND SIGNAL.	12.	21.	2. 17.	21.		(12)	
137	22.	UP STARTING.	8.	22.	17. (9 (9) 11 (11) 12 (12))	22.	WEST MEON		
237	23.	UP HOME.	11. 14.	23.	2.	23.			(14)
S	24.			24.					

COMMUTATOR OF TABLET INSTRUMENT TO WICKHAM
TURNED TO TABLET "OUT" Nº 18 "FREE".

104. - *A wonderful portrayal of No. 30726 shunting the yard at West Meon 28 December 1954 - the same engine is seen in the sequence of images at the top of the page opposite, all taken on the same day with the same train.. Clearly shunting was in progress as the brake-van and two open wagons remain on the running line. Of interest in this view, but perhaps seen more clearly in No. 108 opposite, is the shine on the surface of all the rails, including those in the yard. Clearly freight traffic at least was still at a reasonable level.*

Bluebell Railway Archive / J J Smith 5-114-6

Top, left to right - 105., 106., & 107.
All 28 December 1954.
Bluebell Railway Archive /
J J Smith 5-114-7, 5-114-5, and 5-114-8

Right - 108. - It is matter of regret that whilst, as can be seen, various passenger tickets have survived, nothing has been found reference the goods workings - wagon labels etc. The station accounts books and goods office receipts / ledgers would have provided a wonderful source of information, yet upon closure all would have been bundled into crates and taken for storage. There is little doubt that years later they were destroyed. No 30726 is seen again, this time four days later on 1 January 1955 again with the daily down goods. At this time this was a Basingstoke based engine so it would be interesting to know the circular route taken to involve it in freight on the Meon Valley! With two freight trains in the station, the time would have be between 1 and 2 pm. Freight traffic would be despatched either north or south usually dependent upon its ultimate destination but would also be subject to re-sorting at locations such as Southampton, Portsmouth, Guildford, Eastleigh and Basingstoke.

Denis Cullum 2358

Top - 109. - *From the down platform, a posed view. (The identity of the girls is not known.) The sign proclaims 'Droxford for Hambledon' although it must be doubted how much if any traffic was generated to or from this location. Compare the view with Nos. 29 and 31 concerning the growth that has occurred over five decades. The goods shed had once stood almost behind the signal box.*

Rod Blencowe 31508

Bottom - 110. - *The daily up freight arrives at Droxford whilst the southbound passenger service waits in the platform. 28 December 1954. Just visible on the side of the coach is a board carrying the name of the destination station of the train.*

The Transport Treasury / Leslie Freeman F1404

Top - 111. - *The south end of the yard at Droxford On the extreme left is the down line towards Mislingford and Wickham: next to it is the up line, whilst on the right is the entrance into the yard and its head-shunt - officially 'Up siding No. 2'. Just visible in the distance is the up home signal, 237 yards from the signal box. It was this signal that was altered in 1943 as per the note accompanying the signal box diagram. Note the old type of ground signal, replaced some time after 1949: see Nos. 104, 105 & 107.*

Bottom - 112. - *No. 30055 and the spare Eastleigh push-pull set, No. 662, on the 1.40 pm to Fareham, leaving Droxford, southbound, 1 January 1955. After a 40 chain curve immediately south of the station, the line straightens and drops as it does so - hence the up siding is laid on level ground, this portion of the running line having concrete sleepers. The coaching stock is stored on 'Up siding No. 2', a common practice both here and at Privett. In spring-time it would hauled out, serviced and be made ready again for extra summer traffic on the Southern Region. This was also the siding used by Mr. Churchill in 1944. (A recently found book on local Hampshire history suggests Mr Churchill's train may have taken shelter on occasions in the tunnels on the MV line. This must be open to doubt due to the limited time it remained at Droxford and the need for telephone communication at all times.)*

Denis Cullum 2360

MISLINGFORD

Three miles south of Droxford (and one mile north of Wickham) was Mislingford Siding. Facilities here mirrored those at Farringdon although one obvious difference was that no public passenger halt was ever provided. Again like Farringdon, a 4-lever ground frame was provided, this was released by inserting the single line tablet for the Droxford to Wickham section.

Top - 113. - Looking south towards Wickham, 1 January 1955. The sidings were laid on a brief portion of level track which otherwise dropped on both sides. A goods shed, of similar style to that at Farringdon, had originally been provided here, but that was destroyed in a fire at the adjacent timber yard in 1938. Two railway cottages were built, these may be seen in distance - alongside is a water tower the supply being raised by a wind pump. (Why the railway should have deemed it necessary to provide staff accommodation is unclear. Possibly in the earliest days there was a shunter based here, with the other cottage let to a member of the track gang. It is believed as many as four staff cottages may have originally been provided at Farringdon.) Ground signals were originally provided at Mislingford, but these were removed in May 1945. The name of the location appears on a board above the front windows. Denis Cullum 2361

Bottom - 114. - This time the view is looking north with a wooden hut of unknown purpose visible nestling against the trees. An additional siding terminating near to this hut was provided at some stage - possibly during WW2 - it was taken out of use on 11 January 1948. During WW2 a temporary wooden platform was provided on the running line to serve men from the Canadian Army who were camped in the nearby Forest of Bere. Much wartime traffic was also dealt with at Mislingford, with tanks to be used for D-day stored on specially built concrete bases. War Office records show that around D-Day nearby Droxford would often despatch one train daily loaded with 'stores'. This may well refer to the Mislingford traffic although the same records refer to 'Shipment from USA forces.'. The paperwork gives Droxford a location code of 'UL' with the traffic reported as leaving daily at 8.00 am and limited to 40 wagons. Destinations were either Southampton, Poole, Plymouth or Fowey. In the case of the last two named, an arrival time, part way, at Exeter St Davids and St Budeaux (Plymouth) is given, 4.20 pm and 8.30 pm. respectively. On most occasions the trains ran to time, helped by a steady 15 mph schedule. Research by Denis Tillman indicated tanks from Mislingford were also despatched to Gosport and then sent out from Stokes Bay. 1 January 1955. Denis Cullum 2362

WICKHAM

115. - *North through Wickham on 31 May 1952. This was the only one of the five stations on the line to be built on a straight section of track although the whole site was still on a falling gradient south towards Knowle, hence the provision of a long lay-by siding to the right on the running line. A railway vehicle of some sort may be seen stabled on this in the far distance. Perhaps indicating its potential importance as the largest settlement on the route, a sign was hung under the canopy immediately adjacent to the exit from the booking hall on to the platform. This directed passengers for down trains to the board crossing at the north end of the station in order to cross the line. As befitted the rural railway, one can do no better than to recall the story of the mother and daughter who made a regular journey from Knowle Halt to West Meon. With no ticketing facilities at Knowle, the practise was for mother to alight briefly at Wickham and visit the booking office. This was successfully undertaken several times - until the day when the train left with mother still in the booking hall and daughter on the train - by now rapidly disappearing north. Frantic whistling and waving had the desired result, the guard noticed and stopped the train with his brake, which now proceeded to reverse gently back into the platform. Apologies were made all around before setting off again. Such was life on the Meon Valley Railway, it could never have happened on the main line. 31 March 1952.*

This page: Nos. 116 and 117. - Christmas at Wickham - well winter at least. The date is unknown although it is certainly pre closure. (The 'Southern Railway' poster boards which are certainly pre 1948 are no help as they remained in place into BR days.) Some traffic, road and foot at least has passed whilst in the lower view, there is evidence of some pedestrian passage taking what was an exposed walk towards the end of the platform and perhaps the board crossing to the down platform. On a day such as this the inside of the signal box would be warmest place, a fire burning in the stove. Certainly more so than the booking hall, whose lofty ceiling and entrance / exit doors either side made it a chilling space.

Opposite - The second of the signal box diagrams to have survived. As with that at Droxford, this has a 1948 date yet is drawn in a different style. (The puzzle is why both should be re-drawn in 1948, certainly not just because the name on the top had changed from Southern Railway to British Railways. Usually diagrams were only re-drawn when a change was made to the layout - a minor change might even see a piece of paper pasted over the earlier feature.) Whatever, this again shows a 24 lever frame with the distant signals now fixed and their respective levers spare. Normally a train would not be allowed to pass the up starting signal, No. 3, and proceed on to the single line unless it was in possession of the single line tablet. However, this would have restricted shunting somewhat and so in the absence of an advanced starting signal, the 'Special' note at the base of the diagram will be seen and applicable to the ground signal (No. 18) for leaving the yard. Clearly most of the features had been copied from an earlier drawing as the passenger footbridge is also shown.   Pat Butler

BRITISH RAILWAYS   SOUTHERN REGION

Nº 625.

MEON VALLEY Rᴸʸ
WICKHAM

MEON

1069 YDS TO SIGNAL BOX.

KNOWLE JCT.

UP PLATFORM

UP SIDING

UP LINE
DOWN LINE

DOWN PLATFORM

DROXFORD

DOWN SIDING

SIGNAL BOX

1073 YDS TO SIGNAL BOX.

MECHANICAL LOCKING

DISTANCES IN YARDS FROM SIGNAL BOX	Nº	DESCRIPTION	RELEASED BY	WORK	LOCKING
S.	1			1	
223	2	UP HOME	7	2	9. 11. 21. 23.
57.	3	UP STARTING	13	3	11.
S.	4			4	
S.	5			5	
S.	6			6	
203.	7	F.P.L. ON 8.		7	8.
203.	8	UP LOOP POINTS		8	7
58.134	9	DOWN LINE TO UP SIDING POINTS		9	2. 13. 11. 12. 23.
S.	10			10	
76 142	11	UP SIDING TO UP LINE POINTS.	13	11	2. 3. 9.
86.143	12	DOWN SIDING POINTS		12	9. 23.
192.	13	DOWN LOOP POINTS.		13	9. 14.
192.	14	F.P.L. ON 13.		14	13
S.	15			15	
S.	16			16	
52.	17	DOWN LINE TO UP SIDING OR DOWN SIDING GROUND SIGNAL	9 OR 12	17	20. 21. 22.
74.	18	UP SIDING TO UP LINE GROUND SIGNAL	11	18	19
144.	19	UP LINE TO UP SIDING GROUND SIGNAL.	11	19	18.
136.	20	UP SIDING TO DOWN LINE GROUND SIGNAL.	9	20	17
145.	21	DOWN SIDING TO DOWN LINE GROUND SIGNAL.	12	21	2. 17.
140.	22	DOWN STARTING	8	22	17. (9. 12 B.& F.)
211.	23	DOWN HOME	14	23	2. 9.12.
S.	24			24	

ELEVATED FRAME.
Nº 6 TABLET TO KNOWLE JCT & DROXFORD.
ALL POINTS MECHANICALLY DETECTED.
F.P.L.S. STAND NORMALLY OUT.
WHITE LIGHT GROUND SIGNALS - 17 18 19 20 21.

ELECTRICAL LOCKING

WORK	RELEASED BY	LOCKING
3	TABLET BEING "OUT" TO DROXFORD	
18	TABLET BEING "OUT" TO DROXFORD	
22	TABLET BEING "OUT" TO KNOWLE JCT	

SPECIAL :- THE LOCK OF 18 CAN BE LIFTED OUT WHEN TABLET IS "IN" AT DROXFORD.

Top left - 118. - *The goods yard extended some distance back from the running lines - probably the longest goods sidings at any of the stations. The original goods shed and crane may be identified, whilst a number of additional storage sheds were later provided. Most were in similar corrugated cladding. Notice the discarded metal sleepers by the trackside, the only evidence these items were used this far south.* David Ballard

Top right - 119. - *From the south end on 27 January 1955, what appears to be the down daily goods waits by the signal box. Station Road, leading to the main building, may be seen through the trees on the left whilst out of sight to the left was the goods shed. The down starting signal stands 'on' with alongside a notice warning passengers "Not to trespass - penalty 40/-".* Denis Cullum 2386

Left - 120. - *The buildings at Wickham on 27 January 1955. The station building was in the same orientation as those at Privett and Droxford, whilst the yard facilities and access were also similar to those elsewhere.*

Denis Cullum 2389

121 and 122. - *In March 1933, official records refer to the installation of a 'Key Occupation Wire' between Butts Junction and Wickham. No cost is given although an exact length, 20 miles and 840 yards long was noted! The purpose of this was the introduction of motorised gangers trolleys on the MV line, a system already used widely by the Great Western, less so by the London & North Eastern, and only sporadically by the Southern. Basically, by giving the permanent way gang a motorised trolley (behind which could be towed a small trailer on which tools and equipment might be carried) the men could reach their place of work quicker. That way time would be saved compared with walking. The result was fewer men could cover a greater distance and economy in manpower effected. (Hence the comment at Nos. 80 and 91 where one gang covered from Butts Junction to West Meon. It is likely a second gang, based at Wickham, had responsibility from this point to Knowle Junction. Previously there would have been men at each station.) To operate the system and place a trolley on the track, the ganger first had to liaise with the signalman, the rule book uses the phrase, "arrive at a clear understanding" as to how long the line might be occupied before a train would be due. If going through from one station to another (excluding Privett) then the single line tablet might be used. Normally though, work would be 'mid-section' and for this purpose and with the consent and co-operation of the signalman at either end, an 'occupation key' was withdrawn and issued to the ganger. This would lock the tablet instruments so that no tablet could be withdrawn - and of course no train could enter the section without the tablet. The ganger could then work in safety without the need for flagmen, more men thus available for the work whilst mobility meant they could cover a greater distance. When a train was due, the ganger, plus some of the men, would travel to the nearest 'run-off' point: these were known to him, and consisted of a set of rails set at 90° to the running line. Here the trolley could be manhandled by four men clear of the line - hence the lifting handles seen - there was a handle on each corner. With the trolley safely clear, the occupation key would be reinserted into a machine within the trolley hut and a telephone call made to signalman. The single line could now be worked as usual. When the train had passed the co-operation of the signalmen would allow the occupation key to be withdrawn again and the trolley could be put back on the track. Notice in the lower illustration the telephone just visible on the right hand wall of the hut. Only one trolley would exist per section. The ganger might also use the trolley for general inspection purposes. Examples of the trolley huts are seen in several of the photographs (Nos 47, 58, 69, 98) whilst not shown was one which stood just off the north end of the up platform at Droxford. At the stations the occupation key instrument was in the signal box, hence it is not seen here.*

Left - 123. - *Push-pull Set No. 4 being propelled by No. 30054 near Wickham forming the 1.30 pm Alton to Fareham service. 27 January 1955.*
Denis Cullum 2385

Top right - 124. - *The end of the line at Knowle Junction. The Meon valley route diverges off to the right, straight ahead is the line towards Botley and behind that from Fareham. As opened in 1903, the MV line joined a conventional main line although changes, consequent upon the opening of the 'Fareham Deviation' route from October 1904 and the singling of the route through the Fareham tunnels, resulted in a number of alterations. Between 1907 and 1921 for example MV trains were the only ones able to use the Fareham tunnels, although after this date and up to 1962, the tunnels were worked as a bi-directional single line, with the junctions seen able to use by either MV or Eastleigh trains. Knowle Halt was some little distance behind the photographer on the right hand side. Notice in the 'V' of the junction yet another trolley hut. 27 January 1955.*
Denis Cullum 2382

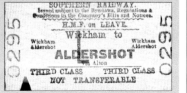

"It is with regret we record the death of Miss. I H Bettesworth, a clerk on the Meon Valley line, who was very well liked by both passengers and staff.

"Miss Bettesworth, who was often seen with her dog, spent practically the whole of her railway career at stations on the Meon Valley line, starting at Droxford in 1925, being transferred to West Meon in 1935 and to Wickham in 1950.

"With the closure of a portion of the line in 1955 she was transferred to Gosport."

(From the 'BRITISH RAILWAYS MAGAZINE' Southern Region, Vol. 3 No. 3 March 1956.)

125. - *And so to Fareham the start and end of the journey for many Meon Valley trains. Some of course would continued straight ahead to Gosport, others would take the sharp curve to the left for Portsmouth, although it was is the bay on the left that we see this particular service. Although the station remains open today it is not a railway station but a 'train station', a media change altered simply because the original phrase had been in use for over 150 years and was considered old fashioned. Old fashioned to and similarly discarded is the line to Gosport, the goods shed and of course the train to Alton. Justification for closure of the MV was given with the provision of an alternative bus service between Fareham and Alton - also long since abandoned, whilst there is some irony now with Hampshire County Council producing a booklet for residents in the Meon Valley villages entitled 'Train and Bus services in the Meon Valley' - **WHAT TRAINS!** 23 July 1952   Terry Cole*

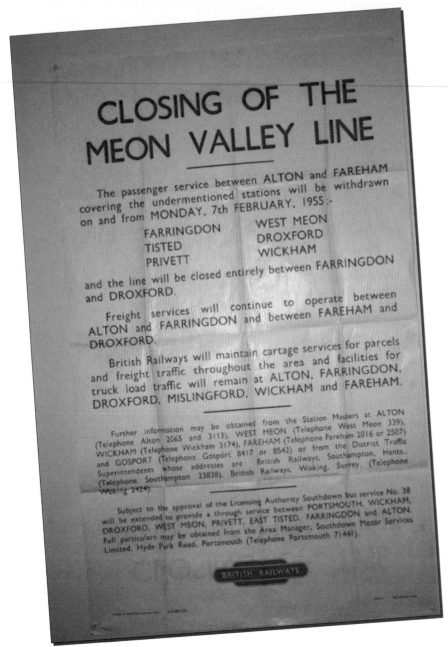

CLOSING OF THE MEON VALLEY LINE

The passenger service between ALTON and FAREHAM covering the undermentioned stations will be withdrawn on and from MONDAY, 7th FEBRUARY, 1955 :-

FARRINGDON	WEST MEON
TISTED	DROXFORD
PRIVETT	WICKHAM

and the line will be closed entirely between FARRINGDON and DROXFORD.

Freight services will continue to operate between ALTON and FARRINGDON and between FAREHAM and DROXFORD.

British Railways will maintain cartage services for parcels and freight traffic throughout the area and facilities for truck load traffic will remain at ALTON, FARRINGDON, DROXFORD, MISLINGFORD, WICKHAM and FAREHAM.

Further information may be obtained from the Station Masters at ALTON (Telephone Alton 2065 and 3113), WEST MEON (Telephone West Meon 339), WICKHAM (Telephone Wickham 3174), FAREHAM (Telephone Fareham 2016 or 2507) and GOSPORT (Telephone Gosport 8417 or 8542) or from the District Traffic Superintendents whose addresses are British Railways, Southampton, Hants., (Telephone Southampton 23838), British Railways, Woking, Surrey, (Telephone Woking 2424).

Subject to the approval of the Licensing Authority Southdown bus service No. 38 will be extended to provide a through service between PORTSMOUTH, WICKHAM, DROXFORD, WEST MEON, PRIVETT, EAST TISTED, FARRINGDON and ALTON. Full particulars may be obtained from the Area Manager, Southdown Motor Services Limited, Hyde Park Road, Portsmouth (Telephone Portsmouth 71441).

BRITISH RAILWAYS

Officially the end of the Meon Valley line came in 1955. But four years earlier the signs were present; restrictions placed on the availability of cheap-day return tickets in addition to the obvious reduction in the actual number of services.

From Fareham, and indeed Gosport, rail travel via the Meon Valley was still used by some to and from Waterloo, although from Gosport at least the journey time could be reduced if a short trip was taken across the harbour to reach Portsmouth.

Post-war the gradual progression of the motor car from a luxury enjoyed by a few to a more general means of transport also hastened the demise of the line. With a limited and to some unattractively timed service, rail travel was seen as inconvenient. There were also those who recalled the incessant delays of the war years, the national service the railway had rendered at that time quickly forgotten. The restriction to four trains each way might have reduced the cost of train running, but it did little to reduce the overall cost of maintenance: and the MV line with its tunnels, steep cuttings and embankments and viaduct as West Meon was expensive to maintain. Earth slips were not uncommon. Whether the condition of the viaduct at West Meon was a factor may only be guessed at, Ray Stone in particular refers to corrosion having eaten away at the metal by the time it was demolished.

In 1954/55 there was also no generally available alternative to steam on the non-electrified lines of the Southern Region. Electrification was probably never considered, certainly not in the 1950s. Whilst diesel railcars operated successfully on the Western Region, these were to a 1930s design, already outdated, and unlikely to be multiplied elsewhere. Although it is a fact that the diesel unit was just over the horizon, it is very doubtful it would have altered history.

Closure was announced for February 1955. Objections via a public meeting in Alton and the National Farmers Union came to nought. The subsequent Transport Users Consultative Committee enquiry was denounced a sham by the Chairman of the Droxford RDC. "The result was a foregone conclusion, as the contract for taking up part of the track was already let in December 1954". (In the event the track was not removed until some time after closure.) Whatever, according to BR closure would effect a saving of £39,000 pa, this by the removal of all passenger workings and complete abandonment between Droxford and Farringdon. But the last train did not run on 5 February 1955, nor was it the enthusiast's special of the following day. And a train did reach Privett some weeks later - and there would be much excitement at Droxford when steam returned, albeit briefly, in the 1960s, and…………. .

(PART 3, the final instalment in the history of the MEON VALLEY RAILWAY, covering the years from 1955, will be available in January 2013.)